CAREERS IN
MARKETING,
PUBLIC RELAT
AND ADVERTI

CAREERS IN **MARKETING, PUBLIC RELATIONS AND ADVERTISING**

Felicity Taylor

Fourth Edition

KOGAN PAGE
CAREERS
SERIES

First published in Great Britain in 1980 by
Kogan Page Limited, 120 Pentonville Road,
London N1 9JN.
Second edition 1983.
Third edition 1987.
Fourth edition 1990.

British Library Cataloguing in Publication Data
Taylor, Felicity, *1934–*
Careers in marketing, public relations and advertising. - 4th ed.
1. Great Britain. Marketing 2. Great Britain. Advertising 3. Great Britain. Public relations
I. Title
658.8′00941

ISBN 1-85091-721-3

Typeset by DP Photosetting, Aylesbury, Bucks
Printed and bound in Great Britain by
Richard Clay (The Chaucer Press), Bungay

Contents

Introduction

This book is intended to give young people leaving school or college some idea of what careers in advertising, marketing and public relations would be like, and how to go about entering them. Part 1 explains what working in these occupations involves, and the kind of people employers are looking for, together with a guide to salaries and prospects. Part 2 lists courses and qualifications relevant to the various jobs, and tells you how to apply for them.

Many young people complain about the lack of advice and information on these careers, perhaps because careers advisers and teachers are only too aware of the difficulties facing entrants to such competitive spheres. But marketing as a whole is a skill that the British are at last beginning to take seriously, and to appreciate that it is no good making excellent products if people are not persuaded to buy them. So opportunities for young people do exist, in an industry that is more likely to expand than contract.

One marketing man suggested that another reason for the dearth of advice was a feeling among some members of the teaching profession that, somehow, careers in 'selling' were not quite socially respectable - insufficiently idealistic. Certainly, there would be little point in entering these careers if you were fundamentally opposed to a capitalist or mixed economy. The same applies if you do not believe (as many marketing people would claim) that consumer choice, which depends on advertising and marketing, is a significant constituent of a free society, as well as the best way of ensuring improvements and efficiency in all aspects of manufacturing goods and services.

Of course, people of all shades of political opinion can be found in any agency or company; but you would not expect to be happy in your work if it grossly offended your principles.

When it comes to preparing yourself for a career in any of these fields, different people will give different, often contradictory, advice. Oddly enough it is often the people who pride themselves on having made it from messenger boy to managing director who are the most insistent on the need for proper qualifications. Others may be more dismissive about specialist courses. It certainly pays to shop around for courses in this area as in any other. Do your best to make sure that the certificates you hope to gain are well regarded and relevant to your aims. A film school graduate may find it easier to obtain a job, however lowly, than an unqualified school-leaver. But in the end, however you manage to enter, it is your own wit, effort and enthusiasm that will enable you to reach the top.

Everyone stresses the need for hard work, conscientiousness and dependability under stress. The industry moves at such a pace that unreliability is a dangerous hazard, and anyone showing signs of it is soon dispensed with, whatever his or her background. So don't go into these careers under the impression that you are in for a life of expense account lunches and trips to exotic locations. With any luck you will get your share of those, but sandwiched between thick slices of exhausting, unremitting, stress-inducing, often frustrating hard labour.

Part 1

Chapter 1

What Are Advertising, Marketing and Public Relations?

Introduction

Whether you work in advertising, marketing or public relations, or in one of the many allied jobs, your basic purpose is the same: you are trying to move and improve goods and services. On the whole, the public is very conservative; it is suspicious of new products and new ideas and it needs to be persuaded to try them. The best product will fail if people do not know how and where to buy it, or have never heard of it. The competition among various manufacturers helps to raise the standard of goods on the market.

All the advertiser can do is persuade consumers to try a product once. If it doesn't live up to the promises made, or if it fails to meet the need for which customers purchased it, they will not buy it a second time. This is where the market researcher and advertising planner are important. It's up to them to see that expensive mistakes are avoided, because if there is something wrong with a product or with the way the product is presented to the public, it is very difficult to eradicate that bad impression.

You could define the work as finding out what the customers want and then selling it to them; in other words, acting as a go-between for the person who manufactures a product and often the retailer who sells it as well as the customer who finally purchases it. The scale of a firm's marketing operations may vary, from one executive with a secretary/personal assistant, to a large department of a multinational company. Advertising may consist of a display ad in the local paper, or the kind of budget that boosts Saatchi and Saatchi's profits to well over £100 million a year. But the problems remain the same: how to ensure that the public will want the goods the firm is producing. And the term 'goods' is not limited to manufactured goods such as washing machines or soap powders. It can also mean books, clothes, jobs, and services of all kinds from banking to holiday travel.

Whatever the scope of the operation, four main functions are involved to a greater or lesser degree:

1. *Information and Research.* Research and analysis into trade, consumer and advertising trends; finding out what competitors are doing and analysing the firm's own operations. Keeping up to date with product development, in the firm and in the industry at large at home and abroad; collecting information about sales and monitoring the firm's performance in the market; studying export markets.
2. *Product Planning.* Making sure that the products match the consumer's needs, and that the company continues to produce a range of products or services to fulfil future needs, always remembering David Bernstein (one of the legendary figures of creative advertising), who said, 'There may be a gap in the market, but is there a market in the gap?'
3. *Sales and Distribution.* Apart from direct selling and distribution, which is not covered in this guide, this involves analysing sales and returns and sales forecasts, and merchandising, often in very elaborate detail. For example, information is available about how housewives shop in supermarkets, the order in which they make their purchases, often buying the staple everyday goods first and leaving the more interesting buys to the end. All of this has to be taken into account when marketing a product.
4. *Advertising and Promotion.* Advertising to the consumer in all media: press, TV, cinema, radio, posters etc. Consumer promotions: offers, coupons, competitions, display material. Trade promotions: incentive schemes for company salesmen and for retailers, sales conferences. Public relations to promote company and product images with consumers and the public at large.

Advertising Agencies

The main job of the advertising agency is to produce advertising campaigns for its clients. But this isn't simply a matter of devising television commercials and press advertisements. The campaign strategy has to be worked out, and, depending on the scale of the client's own operation, the agency may have to do market research, design packaging and display material and set up special trade promotions all to fit in with the theme of the campaign. The agency then has to buy time and space for the campaign's advertisements to be shown, and organise all the printing and other production processes necessary. The two best known areas of agency work are account management and creative services.

Account Management

This is the section responsible for direct contact with the client, and for looking after his account.

In advertising, 'accounts' do not mean financial accounts reckoned as profit and loss in pounds and pence. An 'account' is the composite term for the work done for one product. So you would talk about the Danish Bacon account, or the Schweppes account. An agency might have several different accounts from one manufacturer, but it will never handle competing products; so no agency could hold both the Shell and the Texaco petrol accounts.

Account executives, responsible to an account director, deal with routine contact with the client, and supervise the progress of the work on the account and its finances. Theirs is sometimes an uncomfortable role, caught between loyalty to the client and the agency. They are blamed by clients who don't like the creative work, and blamed by the creative staff who may feel that their ideas have not been presented properly to the client.

The Creative Department

The creative department is often organised into creative groups, consisting of copywriters and art directors and perhaps producers, and their subordinates. Accounts will be assigned to these groups and the members will work together on producing ideas and copy to fit the creative strategy which has been worked out in consultation with the client. Different strategies and ideas may be tried out and tested by market research before the final advertisements are prepared.

Producers arrange for commercials for TV and cinema to be made. This is usually done by specialist film production companies. The producer has to convey what the artist and copywriter have devised to the director of the film production company, who will then produce the required commercials, usually 15 or 30 seconds long. Production assistants carry out much the same kind of functions as an assistant stage manager in the theatre, ie all the dogsbody work.

Many leading film-makers started off learning their trade in agency creative departments - for example, Alan Parker, David Puttnam and Ridley Scott, to name but three.

These two departments, accounts handling and the creative department, are crucial to the agency's success, because it depends on their skill in finding and keeping accounts.

The Media Department

However, the media services departments are also important because they are responsible for buying time and space in the media, where the advertisements will be displayed, and their skill in negotiating the right purchases can be crucial in deciding the success of a campaign.

The media buying department will have to be aware of all the deals and special offers available in different media, and the scope and coverage of different newspapers and magazines as compared with TV, commercial radio and cinemas. Media buyers have to be tough negotiators to get the best deals for their clients, and have to be able to judge very carefully the state of the media market, and how far ahead they need to make firm commitments to space. Nowadays, much of this information is kept on a computer, so they have to know how to use computerised information.

Very precise and quantifiable information is available about media exposure, and this is popular with clients because at least here they can see what they are getting for the money they are spending. The JICTAR ratings can tell you exactly how many thousand housewives will have the TV switched on at a particular time of day (though there is no way of telling whether they are actually watching the commercials). Other ratings measure readership of the press and radio listeners. An annual index running into nearly 100 volumes can tell you almost everything about who bought what, where and how. You can therefore aim your advertisement specifically at a particular market group.

Other Services

A large agency may also have a research and planning department, in order to have its own sources of information about social and demographic trends and consumer buying patterns. It may also test different campaigns or advertisements, to try to find out whether they are communicating the right message to the right audience. Sometimes this information is bought in from a specialist organisation.

Agencies may have their own art or photographic studio, or they may send out most of their routine artwork and photography. Some of the largest agencies run their own film production units, but most prefer to use the many and varied talents of the independent film production companies. In this way, according to the kind of job to be done, they can then hire the best talent available.

Marketing Departments

The way marketing is organised and the degree of power and influence it has over the operations of the firm as a whole vary a great deal from one firm to another. But most modern organisations give marketing a prime position in the firm's hierarchy. The marketing director in a large manufacturing company, who would have overall responsibility for sales operations, advertising and promotions, marketing information and research, and product planning, would have a seat on the board on equal terms with the production and finance directors.

Under the marketing director there will probably be a number of brand or product managers, who will deal with all these functions for a particular product or group of products, using the resources of the firm's specialist departments, as well as buying expertise from outside organisations. The brand manager, for example, will deal with the account executive in an advertising agency over the day-to-day administration of the advertising, although the marketing director would be called in on major decisions. Depending on the number of products and size of the company there may be assistant brand or product managers, who look after minor products or who assist generally on one major product or product group.

In a small organisation, the marketing specialists would be responsible for all the marketing for the firm's products, planning, designing and producing their own publicity material and dealing with outside agencies and the media. They would probably not be directly involved in management of the organisation, or in product planning.

Marketing a New Product

To give you some idea of how this works in practice, here is a very simplified description of how a new product might be brought on to the market.

Stage One. Through sales and market research, and information from the research and development department, a new hair shampoo is developed by a large cosmetics firm.

Stage Two. The marketing manager invites several advertising agencies to put forward proposals for a campaign to launch the new product, and then attends a presentation at each agency of its ideas. This will have involved the agency in a considerable amount of creative work, preparing a plan of campaign and sample advertisements. The account will then be awarded to the agency which, in the client's opinion, has produced the best ideas and plan of campaign. A new product might have a budget of anything up to £2 million, so it is a coup for the successful agency when it wins a new account.

Stage Three. The agency begins work on turning the proposals made at the successful presentation into a coherent strategy. The art director, copywriter and producer will work together to create press and TV advertisements.

Artists will draw out detailed story boards - frame by frame drawings of the film scripts - and will work on the advertisement layouts, also designing display material for shops to use. The final copy may be prepared for the printer in the agency's own department, or sent out to a specialist print shop.

The creative group's TV producer will commission a film production company to shoot the commercials. The film company will set up the shoot, but the producer will be involved in casting and design, and will represent the agency there. The media buyer will recommend a schedule of purchases of press and TV slots for advertisements, best designed to catch the attention of the customers who are the target audience for the new product.

Stage Four. The marketing director will alert the company sales force to the new product and the advertising campaign. A special sales conference may be set up for which the agency will produce a short film and send a representative to talk about the launch. A competition with prizes, such as a weekend in Majorca, may be offered for the retailer selling most cases of the new product. Retailers are of prime importance in launching a new product, because the public will not be able to buy it if the retailer does not stock it. So retailers have to be convinced that there will be a demand for the new line, and will want full details and information about the launch, particularly the amount of TV and press advertising.

Meanwhile, the public relations people have been hard at work. They have been preparing non-advertising material for sending out to women's page editors, and looking into the possibility of using the product name on public information material, eg posters for secondary school children on hair care. They have organised a press lunch for women's page and women's magazine beauty editors, at which presentation packs of the new product are distributed.

Although this work takes several months, and indeed can be a continuous process over several years, there will be constant pressure from deadlines. All the copy must be approved by the account director and the client, and by the TV authorities, any of whom may request last-minute changes even if they approved the original script. There are deadlines for colour magazines, which go to press long before their publication date, deadlines for daily press advertisements and for TV showings. And although the possibilities for error are enormous, there is no room for carelessness or mistakes - they are too expensive. This is why the ability to work well under pressure is a prerequisite for a successful career in this field.

All advertising and marketing people spend a good deal of their time in meetings, with the client or in the agency, to discuss strategy and ideas. The public might be surprised at the amount of intellectual effort and argument that goes into producing what looks like a very simple idea.

The popular view that they also spend a good deal of time entertaining clients is not altogether wrong. This is interspersed with frantic activity as a deadline inexorably approaches, last-minute changes have to be made and long hours worked, because the press advertisement or the TV commercial must be ready on time and the media will not wait.

Public Relations

Possibly no career is more in need of public relations than the profession itself, as it tends to have a bad image (however unfairly) with the general public. But in spite of the lavish media to which we are all exposed, getting information to people who need it is always a problem, particularly in fields such as local government and the public services. A charity will need to bring home to people the needs of the less fortunate, and how they can be helped. One of the main purposes of public relations is just what it says: to maintain good relations with the public, to ensure that all the different publics affected by a firm's activities will think well of it as a supplier, an employer, an investment opportunity, and as a contributor to the local environment, to national prosperity and to economic development.

Another important role is to inform an organisation's own employees about what the company's aims and objectives are and how it is achieving them. Public relations is not involved in selling the individual product, but in creating a favourable climate in which the company can flourish.

There are two main areas of employment in public relations. You can either be a member of the staff of one organisation, such as an industrial firm, a public company, a charity, or local or national government, or you can work in a public relations consultancy for a number of clients. Public relations firms may be independent, or attached to advertising agencies.

Whether working as a staff officer, or for a consultancy, you will require a range of skills to use in a wide variety of activites. They may include using film, photography, design, layout and print, in the production of brochures and information leaflets and other display material; organising special events, exhibitions, conferences and displays, using all kinds of visual aids; and making sure that government - local and national - and its elected representatives are kept informed about the firm's activities, as well as getting publicity in the media. The public relations officer must have a thorough knowledge of the media and how to use it. He or she must know the right people to talk to in radio, television and the press on a particular subject and how best to approach them.

The public relations officer must also act as a channel of communication back to the client about how the organisation's activities are viewed by the public and how these activities can affect the organisation's image.

Chapter 2

What Kind of People Work in Advertising, Marketing and Public Relations?

Introduction

From the brief descriptions given here, you can see that these are not jobs for people who like a quiet life and a regular routine of office hours. And you will not get far by simply following instructions and working by the book. You have to be good at seizing any opportunities that come your way and making the most of them. There is not much room for diffidence. But selling a product is rather like playing a part on the stage; people who may be diffident about putting themselves forward can often overcome their shyness when acting on behalf of someone else, whether a company, product or an organisation. It is not necessarily the aggressive extrovert who gets on best with other people and maximises resources and opportunities.

You must be able to understand the people who make up the market you are trying to reach, how they react to circumstances, the way of life they prefer, and how they see themselves in relation to others and to society as a whole. Respect for the public's intelligence and capabilities is something everyone in any kind of marketing has to learn very early on, often the hard way through underestimating it. It is no good having a false idea of a gullible public that can be easily led. As one very experienced advertising man put it: 'Consumers are always much more sensible than people in agencies and their clients. They expect advertising to inform them about the product, and complain when it doesn't, and complain even more if they feel let down by it. There is a very tight relationship between the producer and the consumer, and if you get it wrong, you can lose a great deal of money.'

It is of course important to be able to see the potential of new ideas and to put them to good use. But there is more involved than having the ability to think up a great new campaign slogan.

Accuracy and reliability are just as important. It is very difficult to cover up errors, and the responsibility for them is even more difficult to hide. When large sums of money are at stake there is no such thing as an excuse, and anyone who is unreliable will find it hard to survive. Talent and drive are essential but so are the ability to take pains to get things absolutely right, and to be there when you are needed.

Another quality not always associated with creativity is an equable temperament. You have to get accustomed to disappointments and take them philosophically. Your unique new product may be brought out by a competitor before you get it off the production line. A campaign tied in to some public event may turn out to be a fiasco - take, for example, the unfortunate American manufacturers who planned a campaign around the US participation in the Moscow Olympics, only to find that the American team was not allowed to participate.

You may have worked on a new business presentation day and night for a week or more and have come up with what you thought was an inspired solution to a difficult marketing problem, only to see the account go to a pedestrian campaign strategy presented by a rival agency. You have to be able to shrug off these setbacks and begin again on something new and completely different, with undiminished enthusiasm.

It is revealing to talk to successful people in the industry, who tend to play down phrases such as creative flair, inventiveness, brilliance, in favour of comments like, 'Well, it's all common sense really'. That elusive quality called common sense seems to be a kind of practical, rational, unflappable judgement that is not frightened of new ideas but is not likely to go overboard in pursuit of novelty for its own sake. It is in fact so *uncommon* that those lucky enough to possess it or be able to acquire it can always claim high rewards for their services.

Advertising Agencies

The staff of the typical advertising agency are a very heterogeneous group of people, from all kinds of different backgrounds, and it is quite difficult to identify any particular characteristics that make for success. There are, however, some obvious points that distinguish an account executive from a copywriter, or a researcher.

Account Management

This is concerned largely with the ability to get on with others, and to present ideas and strategies clearly and accurately. Acting as a go-between, you have to be able to communicate effectively, without irritating or alienating either the client or the creative department of the agency. You must be methodical, so as to ensure that the work on an account progresses at the right pace and nothing is overlooked. Once the campaign is under way, you have to monitor its success, and, if necessary adjust the strategy accordingly.

Case Studies

Sue, who is now a director of a large London agency, explains how she learned the job.

> As graduate trainees, we had a very concentrated training programme in the first three months. We spent two weeks in each department, which gave us at least a superficial idea of how the organisation fitted together. Also, we had a chance to meet people and find out what they did so we knew whom to go to later on. Every day we had a talk from a senior member of staff on a particular topic, anything from a philosophical discussion on creativity to a technical explanation of production or media. So there was a mixture of practical experience and classroom teaching.
>
> After three months, I was assigned to an account group, given a couple of small accounts, and began learning how to do the job. It's a business where you continue learning long after any formal training has ended, I would say for at least five or six years. There are so many different jobs to do and tasks to perform.
>
> It's an elitist business in lots of ways, and there is no doubt that graduates have the edge. They are expected to move fast into positions of responsibility. In a few months, I was given a blue chip (big spending) account. I left that agency after about 20 months, for the usual reason – I thought I wasn't getting paid enough. I stayed for eight years at the next agency, a long time for this business, but it was an agency where people tended to stay. Then I moved here as a director.
>
> You could say that there are three main aspects to account-handling: the salesmanship function, co-ordination and liaison, and, at the highest level, acting as a kind of marketing consultant to the client. As this last depends on authority and experience, it goes with seniority. The ability to sell is a knack; either you have it or you don't and it doesn't depend so much on expertise. The administration and control functions are largely mechanical and usually devolve on the junior members of a group, because this is relatively manageable even when you haven't much experience. There is no direct and clear line

of responsibility, however. When you have a team of three people, one senior one middle and one junior, somehow the work gets shared out between them almost in a mystical way - it gravitates to the right person. As you gain experience, you acquire more responsibility by showing competence in handling the work and grasping opportunities as they arise. It is evolutionary; there is no promotion ladder with clearly defined steps upward.

How you spend your time depends so much on the kind of account you are working on. Some of the very large companies work in a highly structured, formal way; a retail account would be quite different, or you might be working on a small, fussy account that required a lot of detail. A number of things are probably going on at the same time. You could be in the middle of initiating a new piece of creative work, collecting information from the client, processing a brief through agency meetings for the creative staff, clearing a piece of finished work. Any amount of co-ordination and peripheral activities would be going on at the same time: for instance chasing up research, evaluating it, presenting it to the client, analysing market data for the client, shunting paperwork around.

One of the advantages of the job is that in the course of a day it can vary from extremely stimulating and demanding work to very mundane tasks. Now that I have a more senior post, I seem to spend more time in meetings, but I suppose that is a common complaint. I do most of my 'real' work on *ad hoc* projects like new business presentations. The day-to-day running of accounts gets left to other people.

What people in marketing and account handling need is 90 per cent common sense and 10 per cent experience, and this ability to use common sense is what's important, not paper qualifications. That's why I think it best to get in on some kind of graduate scheme, especially if you are aiming high. You can start at the bottom, but it can be very slow progress. Once you are in, the golden rule is to do everything you are asked to do the way you are asked to do it. If you don't understand, ask. If you don't agree, discuss it. But don't go away and do something different because you think you know better. At the beginning you don't. It is all much more complicated than you imagine. Try to do everything as well as you possibly can, even if it is only pouring out the coffee. Advertising is a meritocracy in the best sense of the word, a business where if you work hard and are good at what you are doing you will be noticed and rewarded, unlike some other professions. There are not many good people whose light gets hidden under a bushel. It's an interesting job, it's well paid and it's great fun. What more can you ask?

Peter, who has just joined an agency, looks at the same job with the eye of a beginner.

After leaving school I worked for a chemical company for three years and then as a sales representative until I came here. I wanted to come into advertising for a number of reasons. I had been rather frustrated by my progress in the chemical firm, too much of dead men's shoes. I don't mind some drudgery, but obviously I didn't want a boring job for the rest of my life. I enjoyed part of working as a sales rep, particularly the client contact, but what I disliked intensely was driving around all day; I felt as though my mind was being strangled. Advertising is more likely to accept people like me with a wide variety of experience, so I compiled a list of agencies to write to from copies of *Campaign*, and books about the business, and they took me on here.

I didn't want to be a copywriter, I can't draw, and I thought account handling was the right field for me. It's pretty central, and provided you join an agency where there are not strict demarcation lines, and you have a creative-minded account director, it's not as clerical a job as some people tend to think. You can have the best of copywriters and art directors, but if you can't stimulate the interest of the creative team, the work won't be good. I don't see an account handler as someone who just keeps the client happy. If you go to a doctor you expect him to tell you things about yourself that you don't know, and similarly, if an advertiser comes to us, he is buying our expertise, we ought to be able to show him a thing or two. That's what he pays us for.

Talking to people has not encouraged me to want to be in one of the agencies at the very top of the league, not because it is so competitive, but because I imagine there are so many people there that you could lose your identity. This place is small enough for that not to happen, but it's growing fast enough to be exciting.

I hope to be an all-round account handler, and in my first job I am getting experience in retail, corporate work, package goods and a government account, the whole thing. I feel sorry for someone in my position in another agency who might become stuck on just one kind of account and gain no other experience. I didn't have a fixed idea of what the inside of an agency would be like. But I was quite surprised by the numbers of people of the same age and with similar experience as in the companies I'd worked for before. I find that very encouraging, because if I am in this industry for good, as I hope, I wouldn't want to think I'd be in the dole queue at 40.

Also, the fact that people stay here a long time makes a difference to the relationships. Suppose you go to a production man and say, 'I really need a favour, we've got to have this done tonight'. If you have only been there a couple of months and at four or five agencies before that, he is not going to be as understanding as he would with someone he's known a long time. There is a man in the media department who has been in the industry for years. They all tease him about his age because he is over 50, but he must be one of the best press buyers in London. The other day one of our big accounts wanted to mount a huge extra campaign at very short notice, and the department had all the space booked for *that* week within hours. It was remarkable, but if you want to do well in advertising, you have to be able to cope with that kind of last minute panic.

Creative Work

This is more about developing ideas than about originality, because the original concept goes through so many changes and modifications. This is one of the reasons why several different people often lay claim to being the person who invented 'Guinness is good for you' or any other famous slogan. By the time an idea has been wrangled over by the writers, artists, TV people, account directors and clients, it may be very different from the original.

Some years ago, there was fairly precise demarcation in an agency between copywriting, film producing, art directing. But at the present time, although people may be taken on as layout artists or trainee copywriters or producers, as they get used to working with creative groups these functions merge together, and there is less distinction between who does what.

This is particularly true in the early stages of planning a campaign or new advertisement. Once the idea is fully thought out it can more easily be split up into component parts, and handed over to less senior people to work on.

Copywriters do not need to be great imaginative writers, but they must have a feeling for words, economy of style, and an endless capacity for saying the same thing over and over in different ways, and over again, without getting bored or boring. They have to be able to understand the people with whom they are trying to communicate, the target audience, and to write for that audience, not for themselves. One very successful creative director put it this way: 'I am very quick to detect self-indulgence in creative work. I know that when a copywriter wants to shock people, he or she is really expressing a dislike for the work or the client. I tend to see so-called creativity as axe-grinding that's more to do with the insecurity of the creator than the desire to do anything new for the brand. If you take responsibility for the brand, are sensitive towards its needs, you don't make that mistake. Suppose you write an ad for an ashtray. When you ask yourself the question, "If an ashtray could speak would it talk like that?", if the answer is "No", then the advertising is wrong. It must speak in the words of the ashtray. If you can make it seem true, that's where the ingenuity and creativity lies, and that's where you have a complex and interesting job to do.'

To become an *art director*, the ability to draw well is not enough; you must also have a feeling for layout and effect, and the ability to translate the creative idea into something like reality.

However, the ability to draw well is important. That may sound obvious, but neat and carefully drawn accurate design to a formula is much more difficult to produce than an 'artistic' picture. Run-of-the-mill illustration, such as storyboards, which are sketch layouts for a series of film shots, and work for animatics, which are a rough presentation of still pictures on film with sound added, to give an impression of what a film commercial would look like, are often put out to specialist studios. 'Good wrists' who can draw what's wanted accurately at short notice, soon make a name for themselves and can earn large sums of money, working all the hours there are.

Case Study

Shan, a young art director describes her working day.

> When I came here, the most difficult thing was getting to know the different departments and who does what. You are expected to know; people forget you still have a lot to learn. I did a lot of work I didn't need to do because of that. Although my college gave me a good grounding in typography and basic design, the approach is so different in advertising. At college we were looking at the total effect, the design as a whole, whereas here, selling is the main aim.
>
> I worked very hard at the beginning, and I was fortunate because people took an interest in me and gave me the chance to prove myself. It would have been easy to sit back and do very little because as a trainee you are in a way superfluous. You have to work hard to show that you have something to offer. Although you must be able to stand up for your own ideas, you have to learn to take criticism, and also to talk to other people in the agency when you get stuck. I was very lucky in the early stages, as one of the art directors asked me to submit ideas for one of the large accounts. I think it was just to give me something to do. Quite unexpectedly, my idea was the one chosen. In the meantime, the man who had given me that chance had left, and I had to see the whole thing through on my own - posters, display, everything.
>
> After I had been here three or four months, they said they would keep me on and find me a copywriter to work with. The first one was asked to leave after three months. She was very talented, and I got on quite well with her, but she didn't have the right approach. That handicapped me for those three months; I have nothing to show for them at all. Now, with a new copywriter, things are going much better.

He is very enthusiastic, which helps a lot. We don't have our own accounts yet, we work on anything that needs doing. When we are given a brief by the accounts people, first of all we discuss it together. As soon as we have some ideas that we think are worth working up, he starts writing copy and I work on the design. Then we talk it through again, and when we get something we think good enough we take it to an internal meeting. We may give it to our studio to draw up properly, or send it out to a specialist firm if it is important and we have the time. You have to find your own way of working, that suits you; there's no one to tell you how to do it.

Today has been very hectic; I had an agency meeting at 9.30 which lasted about an hour, to discuss a brief we were given a few days ago. The client is coming in the day after tomorrow to look at the work. I have to plan a leaflet for the company salesmen about a new product. As I came out of the meeting another account executive caught me and asked me to do a three-page insert for a guidebook, based on a leaflet I worked on a few months ago. This had to be ready for 4 pm tomorrow. I was working on the leaflet, and had sent out the format I liked best to be made up for the client meeting on Wednesday, but it still needed some changes. Then the other exec phoned to say that the insert was needed for a meeting with the client at 5 pm today, so there was a rush to get something ready. But at 5.30, a message came to say that the client wasn't feeling well and would not be coming in till tomorrow.

When there is a panic on, you have as much responsibility as anyone in the agency. People must be able to trust you to get the work done competently in time. I have learned that you have to make things happen; they will not fall into your lap, and even if they do you cannot afford to sit back and enjoy yourself. It is not easy to be successful; it's a lot of hard work, but you can succeed if you have confidence in yourself and your work, and are prepared to get on with it.

The *agency producer's* job is to organise the transfer of all this creative effort into the actual television or film commercial. The first stage is to set up all the preproduction work necessary: choosing a production company, briefing the director, supervising the choice of cast, props, location, wardrobe etc. The producer has to negotiate a quote for making the commercial with the production company, that will allow for the quality of work needed without taking up too high a proportion of the campaign's budget. This has to take into account artwork, artist's fees and repeat fees, recordings, and prints of the final version as well as the production costs of the shoot.

A very important part of the agency producer's job is to select the best production company for the type of film. This means knowing what is going on in the whole field of television production, making judgements about directors, looking at the show reels of many different companies to get some idea of the quality of their work, and keeping an eye open for promising newcomers (who may be less expensive than the established 'names').

Having attended the shoot, which is often long, cold and boring, the producer has to see the film through the remaining stages, the important editing of the final version, the addition of sound, perhaps with the composition of special music tracks. It is astonishing how much work goes into one 15-second commercial.

Information and Planning

This calls for people experienced in research techniques, together with a knowledge and understanding of human nature. It is not just a question of collecting numerical information about buying patterns, incomes and consumer preferences. You must also have an interest in and empathy with consumers in order to be able to interpret their needs and wishes effectively.

Case Study

Mary, an experienced planner, describes what planning means in her big London agency.

> The planner's particular job is to understand the ultimate consumer - who he or she is, how they tick, why they tick that way, where their points of strength and vulnerability lie - and to be able clearly and simply to represent them to the creative department whose ultimate job it is to convince them of something or other. This process demands the gathering together, the interpretation, and the evaluation of information - which can come from any source.
>
> Good planners make good use of information - getting it into the right perspective, knowing when to take it at face value, when to ignore it, when to accept it as gospel. More often than not, the advertising job to be done is to make consumers think differently. All research can do is relay to you the status quo - how it is at the moment. What we have to do is to think in terms of stretching it, changing its shape, *moving* it somehow. We have to step aside from the here and now, and imagine how it can be changed or moulded for future growth and profitability. Knowing how much merit to give such information - and having the courage and conviction to use it merely as a reference point and not a straitjacket - is a fundamental asset of a successful planner.
>
> We also, of course, have a long-term commitment to keep up with what is going on in the outside world in general - on all aspects that

could concern the future prosperity of our clients - and to a certain extent ourselves - like the economy; the availability of packaging materials; changing eating habits, lifestyles etc. At the moment it would be nice if all our clients were in things like pushbikes, pipe lagging, convenience foods, or disposable nappies - all boom products in times of economic recession.

And, of course, we do have to do a lot of advertising development research. We believe that money spent talking to consumers in the early stages of campaign development results in better value than that spent checking it out later.

Marketing Departments

If you want to succeed in a marketing job, you need to be interested in the mechanics of business as well as the conventional marketing skills and market research techniques. You have to be able to understand the production processes involved in your product, or how a particular service is provided; it is also important to have an understanding of salesmanship and sales people, as without their co-operation your efforts will be handicapped.

You must be prepared to work hard at mastering the way in which the company operates, and at acquiring technical information about its products and services. You must also learn as much as you can about the market you are aiming at. You have to be able to understand and use large amounts of data from many different sources, and to be ready to co-operate with staff in other departments and organisations.

It has always been a criticism of British industry that we have good ideas and inventions, but fall down when it comes to capitalising on them. So a marketing expert may have to be very persuasive at putting plans across to senior management, who may still need convincing that marketing is not an optional extra whose budget can be cut in hard times.

You need to be able to take the long view as well as deal with short-term considerations, so that you always have in mind what will be happening to a product in three or four years' time as well as today.

Many of the jobs described in advertising agencies have their counterparts in company marketing departments. For example, school-leavers or graduates taken on as management trainees may be assigned as *assistant brand managers* as their first job. This parallels the work of account executive in an agency and would involve helping to work out the advertising and marketing strategy for the brand, working on packaging and promotion, liaison with the sales force and monitoring sales performance. Brand managers deal with the advertising agency, and with any public relations firm used for their brands.

Depending on how the company marketing functions are organised, you could also work in the advertising or publicity department, carrying out general advertising and publicity duties for the company as a whole or for selected brands or services. Alternatively, you might get a job in the advertising department of one of the media organisations, either dealing with people who want to advertise in that medium, or undertaking marketing work for the newspaper, magazine, or television or radio company itself.

Almost every kind of organisation may employ marketing specialists. The range is enormous.

Case Study

Sally is a brand manager in the cosmetics division of a multinational company. When she left college, she had no professional qualifications in marketing.

> I took a degree in French and Latin at Oxford, having originally thought of doing business studies, but I had decided to keep my options open. When I graduated, I didn't have enough languages to be a successful linguist, but I was attracted by the idea of marketing as a career as it seemed to combine languages with the business studies approach. As I worked for a multinational company I shall have the opportunity to work abroad at some stage. I could, for example, apply for a post in Paris with a good chance of getting a two-year stint there.
>
> At the moment, as a brand manager I've found that the most important part of managing a brand is co-ordination - developing and carrying out the decisions that have been taken at a higher level. You have to co-ordinate every aspect of the marketing of the brand; if the brand manager doesn't do it, no one else will. That means initiating work on the advertising, market research and analysis, the strategic development of the market, the sales estimates, the printing and packaging design and the general financial control.
>
> In theory we are profit responsible and are judged on the profit performance of our brand's year-end figures. But this is difficult in practice as there are so many factors involved. However, we have to administer the brand's budget for promotional expenditure set at the beginning of the year and should be able to turn in a profit figure by the end.
>
> At least half my time is usually spent in administration: queries

from other people, updating estimates, decisions on printing and packaging. For packaging artwork, for example, I have to brief a designer and act as liaison between the designer and the factory. I control the design within the overall strategy that has been agreed.

I report to the marketing manager, who deals with a whole range of cosmetic products. Different managers have different styles of management; some will keep control over every little detail, others will allow you more responsibility.

I'm the brand's representative with the advertising agency, and I have to set up meetings with them and decide what needs to be done. If it's a new campaign, it's up to me to screen the material that comes back from the agency, so in the early stages I have quite a lot of control over which ideas go forward, though the ultimate decisions on advertising rest with the marketing director. I have to discuss all the sales estimates with the sales department and warn them if, for example, a specific promotion is going forward, so that we know what extra sales to expect. Similarly with pricing, I have to assemble a document showing what proportion of the price is spent on promotion within my budget, and I need to have the agreement of the sales department on pricing as they are the market experts, while I am the expert on my brand.

So a lot of time is spent in contact with people in other departments and it's very important to get on well with them. It's very much an all-round job. It's no good being interested only in the creative side because there is such a lot of administrative work. You have to be numerate, and prepared to do a good deal of number-crunching, and churning out of detailed documents. You need to know your own weaknesses, and when to ask for help from the specialists. You are encouraged to fight for your brand, but you have to be able to rise above that and think about the corporate business strategy, the good of the whole group. So you must have the ability to grasp business ideas and feel at home in the business environment.

Our company offers excellent in-house training. In the four years I have been with them, I've been on a financial course, an advertising course and an external market research course, as well as the introductory training course. We're very lucky to receive such good grounding.

Marketing requires a great deal of enthusiasm and energy. To succeed you must be prepared to exert yourself, do unconventional things, be flexible. It's not a job for people who like to do the same thing every day. It's not a specialist job. If you want to succeed, you may have to move out of marketing for a time into sales or planning, or go abroad. It's common to serve as a brand manager in the UK, go abroad as a marketing manager, and then come back to a senior post. You have to be prepared to take jobs abroad when they are available; if the right job comes up in South America tomorrow, you have to seize that chance.

Public Relations

The skills required are very similar to those for the careers already mentioned: a thorough knowledge of the product, an ability to sift and use information from a variety of sources, an eye to the main chance, a readiness to create your own opportunities where they do not obviously exist, imagination and, above all, articulateness - a fluency and clarity in speaking and writing - so that you are easy to understand and compelling to hear.

It is quite difficult to enter public relations without having had some previous experience in a related field such as advertising or journalism. One way in for the new entrant is through information officer work; a job as assistant information officer, classifying and disseminating information about an organisation or company can be very good training for public relations work.

Chapter 3

How to Get a Job

All these careers are popular; they have a certain glamour and offer very good prospects, so there is no shortage of applicants and it can be very difficult to gain entrance into them. Another difficulty is that many firms prefer to employ people with some experience, as they do not have the time or facilities for training. How to obtain the experience is a problem. Most college courses include work experience, but even the colleges have difficulty in arranging this for all their students. You may have to persevere for a long time before you find the opening you want. It may be necessary to begin by taking a job in sales, despatch, or reception, in the hope of moving on to the career that really interests you later. If you show promise and enthusiasm, you stand a good chance, as these professions are looking for new talent and are usually eager to recognise and use it.

Although about 75 per cent of the advertising industry and associated services is concentrated in the London area, most provincial cities and large towns have at least one local advertising agency, and it is worth approaching any in your area. They may not handle the big prestige national accounts, but otherwise they carry out the same range of functions as a London agency.

There are jobs in marketing, and to a lesser extent in public relations, in firms and organisations all over the country.

A good source of information are the various directories and yearbooks used by people in the business, for example:

Advertiser's Annual (June 1989 edition £55 plus £2.50 postage; also covers marketing)
Thomas Skinner Directories, Windsor Court, East Grinstead House, East Grinstead, West Sussex; 0342 326972

BRAD Advertiser and Agency List (subscription £100 a year)
British Rate and Data, Maclean Hunter House, Chalk Lane, Cockfosters Road, Barnet, Hertfordshire EN4 0BU; 01-441 6644

A quarterly list of London and provincial agencies and their accounts.

Creative Handbook (£40 plus £2.50 p&p)
Thomas Skinner Directories, address on page 32

Institute of Public Relations Members' Register (£23.00 annually, free to members)
Institute of Public Relations, Gate House, St John's Square, London EC1M 4DH; 01-253 5151

As you can see, all these books are very expensive, but you should be able to find them in a specialist library, or careers or large reference library, especially in London.

Whatever the particular field of work you want to enter, there are four main ways of finding a job.

Finding a Job

Traineeship Schemes

Many large companies, and a few of the larger advertising agencies, have training schemes for young entrants, either for general management traineeships or specific schemes geared to marketing, advertising etc. Other firms may occasionally offer an individual place. These traineeships are mainly for graduates, though there may be some for people leaving school with A levels. As one media sales executive explained, it is much more difficult nowadays than it used to be to come in without exam qualifications and work your way up. The Institute of Practitioners in Advertising suggests that the best way of finding out about schemes in advertising agencies is to begin by writing to, say, the top 20 agencies and ask if they are offering any traineeships. If you can't find anything, you then work your way down the list of agencies, hoping that something will turn up.

The annual *Directory of Graduate Opportunities*, *GO*, published by Newpoint Ltd, lists the employers who are prepared to take on graduates in different areas of industry; it costs £20 but is available at careers services.

Competition for traineeships in the major companies is very keen, with several hundred applications for a few places each year. Your school or college careers officer, or the local authority careers service, should have full information about them. They will know about local schemes as well as nationally organised ones, and will be able to advise you about your chances of being accepted. You can, of course, write directly to a company to ask for details. The usual formula of these schemes is for trainees to spend perhaps six months getting a general introduction to the company, and then specialise in a particular department or section. Training in the company may be supplemented by day- or block-release to a college to study for formal qualifications.

Job Advertisements

You should study the newspapers and magazines for advertisements. Every Monday, the *Guardian* has a wide range of advertisements for creative, media and marketing jobs. The major specialist papers are *Campaign*, published weekly by Haymarket Publishing Company, 22 Lancaster Gate, London W2 3LY (01-402 4200), *Media Week*, 27-31 Saffron Count, Southfields Industrial Estate, Laindon, Essex SS15 6SS (0268 410181 ext 127) and *Marketing Week*, St Giles House, 50 Poland Street, London W1V 4AX (01-439 9381). These papers also carry advertisements from the many 'headhunters' who operate extensively in the advertising and marketing field. Many senior posts are handled by recruitment agencies, and they may also fill some junior posts. Evening papers may carry advertisements for vacancies for juniors and jobs in studios.

Your nearest central reference library should carry a range of specialist publications, including these.

Graduate Post, published on subscription by Newpoint, carries advertisements of jobs and government-sponsored training programmes for graduates. It comes out once a fortnight, and costs £16.50 for one year, £9.90 for six months, £5.95 for three months. Subscriptions from Newpoint Ltd, Newpoint House, St James Lane, London N10 3DF. It is stocked by college careers services.

Transferring from Another Job in the Same or a Different Firm

This is probably the most common way of getting into public relations, for example, as you usually need experience in other fields, such as journalism. Similarly, many people enter marketing after beginning their careers as salesmen, and it is much easier to get a job in an advertising agency if you can produce evidence of relevant experience elsewhere.

You may be able to get a job as a messenger (especially if you can ride a motor bike) and work your way up, or as a 'gofor' in a film production company – the person who is told to go for anything anyone might happen to need.

It is often said that women can get into more rewarding work by starting in a secretarial or office job. This is to some extent more true of these careers than some others; for example, a secretary to a TV producer in an agency may develop into being an assistant producer. You do have to be very tough and ambitious to break out of the secretarial role, but you probably have to be tough and ambitious to succeed anywhere in these careers. People come into the creative side of advertising from all kinds of backgrounds, usually with some media or artistic connections. There is a lot of luck and some skill in being in the right place at the right time. On the whole, advertising and public relations are fairly small communities and once you are connected with them, even peripherally, you get to know where the jobs and the likely openings are. The same is true of marketing departments in a company; once you are inside the system, you can spot the chances more easily.

Writing in and Asking for a Job

This needs time and stamina, and an inexhaustible supply of stamps, but it is how many young people get their first chance. You pick out the companies in which you are interested, and simply write to the personnel officer in a large firm, or the appropriate director in an agency (you find out who this is by ringing up and asking). The first approach does not have to be a long letter, but it must say something to catch the interest as these people receive many such letters every week.

If you are a student, you can write to ask if they will give you a holiday job, unpaid if necessary, as long as it gives you some experience. You may have to write over and over again, and hope that they will be impressed by your persistence.

Preparing Your Application

However you make your approach to a firm, you must spend some time on preparation. It makes sense to find out as much as you can about the company. What are its major products? What accounts does it handle? What is its marketing or advertising style? Take the trouble to look critically at marketing and advertising techniques. Read the advertising press and see what the trends are. Every year the various advertising associations make awards for the best advertising in different categories, and these are reported in the advertising press. Find out what advertising wins awards and see if you can understand why. For example, the Designers and Art Directors Association, 12 Carlton House Terrace, London SW1Y 5AH (01-839 2964) has an annual public exhibition of the advertising that has won its gold and silver awards. Go and see this if you can, and read about the awards in the specialist press.

If you hope to get employment as an artist, make sure your portfolio contains some work relevant to advertising, so that you can demonstrate that you have thought about the problems and the techniques necessary.

The magazine *Designer* once carried a survey of art directors in London advertising agencies in which they were asked why and how they chose artists and designers. This included some helpful if sharp comments about portfolios. A few good items are better than a mass of mediocre work. Directors appreciated work that showed some understanding of reproductive techniques, and specimens designed as an ad not as a studio picture. Above all, they expected a high standard of presentation and complained about too many boring, slapdash, messy samples of work.

The qualities that most art directors rated the highest, after (predictably) talent, were enthusiasm and interest.

When you are preparing a curriculum vitae, or biographical notes about yourself, your qualifications and experience, you have to make it lively and interesting, but not too long. Do not forget vital details such as your name, address, and a phone number where you can be reached at short notice. Make sure there are no grammatical or spelling errors. Busy people do not have the time to wade through a mass of handwritten, badly laid out, irrelevant details backed up by the publicity leaflet you did for the school production of *Hamlet* five years ago. So get your curriculum vitae typed professionally if you can, and pick the best example of your work, that will reproduce well, and then get good quality copies made of this package. It may cost you a few pounds but it is an investment you should try to afford. Keep a copy handy to refer to in case someone telephones and interviews you there and then on the phone. It is essential to give the impression that you are serious about your application, and have thought carefully about the kind of contribution you could make to the company.

People with a Disability

There is no reason why people with disabilities should not be able to make successful careers in almost any aspect of marketing and advertising, if they have the necessary talents. On the whole, they will probably find less prejudice and discrimination against them than elsewhere. One of the great postwar creative directors was confined to a wheelchair for most of his working life.

Chapter 4

Salaries and Prospects

Introduction

It is probably more difficult to give an indication of what salary you are likely to command and what your careers prospects are for these professions than for any others. It depends so much on your individual talents, on the chances that come your way, and on the economic situation. It is fair to say that in your first job you would probably be getting £9,000 to £15,000 in account handling/planning; £8,000 to £14,000 in a media department; £8,000 to £16,000 in a creative department (1989 figures). You could expect to increase this dramatically after about a year, if you can produce good work during that time. It is customary to improve your salary by changing jobs very frequently in the early stages of your career. If you do well you could be earning £30,000 a year before you are 30. Rather than attempt to describe the great variety of jobs and salaries available, here is a sample of job vacancies taken from *Campaign* and other papers.

The top jobs are seldom advertised, because they are usually filled by word of mouth or through headhunters, at salaries of anything up to £100,000 plus profit-sharing, or even higher.

NB 'Above the line' means advertising, display and media expenditure; 'below the line' (or BTL) means promotional expenditure on coupons, competitions, offers etc; DTP: Desktop Publishing; POS: Point of Sale; OTE: On Target Earnings.

Advertising

Designer/Copywriter, part-time; £8 per hour. A leading hospital management company based in Central London wants to recruit an experienced copywriter/designer to work in-house on a part-time basis. Probably well versed in producing advertisements for a cross-section of clients. Will be responsible for liaising with our consultants to produce advertisements that will secure staff for our major contracts in the Middle East.

Two people: **Art Director.** Strong, original thinker; good put down; exciting talent; creative brain that puts it all into great ads. **Designer**. Works well below-the-line; loves design and print; can take a job through to artwork. Financial rewards and sleepless nights go with the success you'll enjoy and the portfolio you'll create.

Writer. £18,000. London. Direct marketing. Big company. Blue-chip clients. DTP experience. Conceptual.

Senior Copywriter. £18,000. Manchester. Senior writer who revels in words and ideas for top five agency.

Senior Designer. £15,000 to £20,000. Ideas person with good put down and graphic skills to have full responsibility for household name accounts. London W1.

Art Director. £18,000 to £24,000. Across-the-line conceptual and design expertise for WC1 agency. Recruitment experience essential.

Copywriter. c£23,000. South West. TV, press, radio and BTL for a variety of large quality accounts.

Senior Artist/Studio Manager designate. We require a finished artist who takes great pride in producing excellent mechanicals for ads, packaging, brochures and POS material. You will ideally be in your mid/late twenties with 3/4 years' experience.

Senior Account Manager. For rapidly expanding London advertising agency. You will need a minimum of 4/5 years' account handling experience to help us service our ever-increasing and diversifying client base.

Advertising Account Manager. Gloucestershire. £18–£20k. Prestigious full service agency with interesting mix of accounts requires an experienced professional. Excellent communications skills are essential.

Artist All Rounder. There's roughs, finished artwork and layouts to do, freelancers to organise and it all needs doing by yesterday. Call if you think you can cope and have a minimum three years' experience across a range of work. Great working conditions in Victorian house with stream running through the garden in Middx.

Writer for Direct Marketing Agency. c£20k. You've gained experience in direct response writing (above or below the line) and now you're looking to spread your wings. Ideal for someone who has been writing successfully for a couple of years and is keen to develop.

Planning and Media

Planner. Top 10 agency requires a good all rounder, TV planning essential, to work on blue-chip account list. This role is planning oriented and requires involvement in the whole advertising process to include below-the-line activity etc and strategic development of accounts.

Media Sales. We need a dynamic, highly motivated person to start a recruitment venture within an expanding advertising agency. You will be responsible for building and monitoring your client base, marketing the new division and monitoring advertising expenditure.

Ad Manager. Business newspaper of international metal trade. The position calls for someone able to build strong client contact with the journal's worldwide advertisers. Linguistic fluency a help in running a polyglot team. Reports to experienced divisional sales and marketing manager. Around £25K OTE and car.

Display Sales Executive. Basic plus commission equals £16,000 package. Age 22-plus. Central London. High achiever with loads of energy needed in competitive market. Could be career launchpad within company.

Display Advertisement Manager. £15–£18k plus commission. Construction industry journal. Must be successful and ambitious with the ability to sell to both clients and agencies at director level. Management experience and training in display sales desirable but not essential.

Advertisement Sales Assistant. We are looking for an enthusiastic and self-motivating person, probably in their early twenties and educated to at least A-level standard, or possibly with a degree. You would work as part of a team, assisting a sales group in achieving maximum advertising volume and revenue. You will need to be a fast worker, quick-witted, able to work under pressure, yet have a mature personality and be able to get on with a wide spectrum of people. You will be expected to show the ability to advance within the sales structure of the newspaper.

Marketing

Senior Marketing Consultants to join a team of seven consultants working on a wide range of marketing activities, from new product development to business planning. The successful candidates will be good honours graduates, preferably with MBAs, and have at least seven years' good consumer marketing experience gained with a minimum of two major organisations. They will be working at product or marketing manager level, demonstrating their problem-solving and analytical abilities as well as their first-class communication skills. Newcastle. £30k plus car and benefits.

Sales Promotion Executive. £16,000 plus car. Consultancy with many blue-chip clients. Fast-moving environment calls for excellent account-handling skills. Consumer orientated, you will create and develop strategies and enjoy a high degree of autonomy.

Product Manager. The company supplies many high-volume own-label lines to all grocery multiples – some of which are tailormade to meet customer needs. A successful branded range is also in evidence. The PM needs an understanding of trade marketing and liaison with a production unit. £16,500 plus car.

Trade Marketing Manager. Knowledge of major grocery accounts and the management of both branded and own label products are key requirements of the job, so experience in national account selling and marketing would ideally fit the specification for the job. c£23,000 plus car.

Account Director. Hertfordshire-based sales promotion agency needs an experienced account director to strengthen its account handling team. The person must be capable of developing new business as well as expanding activity within existing clients. Previous sales promotion is essential, together with creativity and enthusiasm. c£30,000.

Industrial Product Manager. London. To £17,000 plus car and bonus. To assume full marketing control of a range of garage door and sliding door products. The role encompasses all the elements of the industrial marketing mix and being profit responsible you will have the opportunity to exercise strategic planning, commercial and creative skills. Preferably a graduate, the ideal candidate will be able to point to at least 18 months' sound marketing experience gained within a reputable company. This experience could be gained in a variety of industries as this organisation is more interested in people with good marketing knowledge and excellent interpersonal skills.

Public Relations

Secretary. £10,000 to £12,000 with benefits. The last three secretaries to hold this position are now PR executives! Capable person, preferably a graduate, with good secretarial skills and the ability to prioritise without supervision and cope with lots of pressure. Opportunity to work in an increasingly demanding, yet rewarding environment in computers and telecommunications.

Design Consultancy PR Director. £25,000. The company's work ranges from Corporate Identity to packaging and interior design and their clients are household names. As part of a major marketing drive they want to appoint a public relations director. The position requires a tough, highly motivated, decisive professional who has complete confidence in his (sic) own ability. You should be a skilled writer and 'ideas' person, ideally with a knowledge of the design industry.

Publicity Officer. BBC television drama. Opportunity for experienced journalist. Special responsibility for television drama, particularly the promotion of single films and plays. The primary duties involve writing press releases and arranging press occasions, forging and maintaining close links with programme makers and contributors and acting as spokesperson on relevant matters. You should have at least two years' experience as a publicist or journalist, excellent writing skills and original and innovative promotional ideas, together with the ability to work quickly and accurately, often under pressure. £15,655–£19,863 plus £698pa allowance. West London.

Press Officer. c£11,500. Northampton Borough Council. Journalist needed to help publicise the Council's services and the booming Northampton area. He/she will seek out stories within the Council and turn them into front page news, and will respond quickly and positively to reporters' enquiries. There is also scope for editing and contributing to other publicity material so this is a good career step for someone wanting wide experience in a PR unit. Candidates must demonstrate broad writing skills and have first-hand experience of newsroom practices.

PR Account Executive (minimum one year's experience) and **Junior Account Executive** needed by fast-expanding consultancy to work on mixture of business to business, hi-tech and professional services accounts. Candidates must be prepared to take on responsibility at an early stage. Attitude, approach and enterprise will be highly important. Salary negotiable according to age and experience.

Part 2
Introduction

Success in marketing, advertising and public relations may depend much more on personal qualities than on qualifications, but you still need to look carefully at the opportunities for continuing your education after leaving school, to decide which route to follow.

Part 2 of this book sets out the different kinds of course you can take, and explains how to find out which colleges offer them. Help and advice about courses and qualifications should be available at school or college, or from the local authority careers service. This can be very useful when you are making up your mind about what to do as they know the local educational and employment scene, would be able to advise you about national qualifications and should know something about your own personal interests and capabilities. You have a right to their services - use them.

Addresses will be found in Chapter 11, page 86.

Chapter 5

What Courses and Qualifications are Available

You may prefer to study for a qualification related to careers in marketing rather than an unrelated degree or DipHE course. This section lists some of the types of course and qualification available, and gives a brief description of them.

- University or CNAA degree in media or communication studies or marketing;
- University or CNAA degree in business or management studies with marketing or other appropriate option;
- Diploma of Higher Education with appropriate options, eg art, communications;
- Art and Design courses;
- BTEC and SCOTVEC Certificate and Diploma courses in business or communications studies;
- CAM Certificate and Diploma courses;
- Institute of Marketing Certificate and Diploma courses;
- Other special courses.

University Degrees

If you want to study for a university degree with a marketing, advertising or other appropriate content, you are more likely to find what you want at one of the newer universities, or those with a technological bias. Many of their courses do not follow the traditional single-subject pattern; instead, the course structure consists of a range of options related to a central theme. They may be sandwich courses, where you spend at least one year of a four-year course in employment, related to the field of study.

An example is the course incorporating communications studies at Bradford University, where you apply for a BA course in interdisciplinary studies and choose to specialise in one of five subjects during your final year. These are:

Communications
Literature
Philosophy
Psychology
Sociology

Degrees in business or management studies necessarily cover a wide range of topics, from law and accounting finance to human relations and quality control. When you have been used to studying for the narrowly based A-level exams, you may find the breadth of these multi-disciplinary courses hard to cope with at first, especially as each subject may use different methods and techniques.

In Scotland the broader-based four-year degree course is the normal pattern. Scottish students usually begin the course after taking the Scottish Higher Certificate at the age of 17.

CNAA Degrees

These are the responsibility of the CNAA - the Council for National Academic Awards. Courses are available in polytechnics, colleges of art and design, colleges of higher education, colleges of education, and other specialist institutions. Colleges devise their own syllabuses and exams, and these are vetted and monitored by the CNAA. They tend to have a more practical bias than university courses, and may use project work and continuous assessment, rather than relying on a once-and-for-all exam as a test of students' competence. A number of colleges offer modular courses, where you can choose your own programme of studies from a wide range on offer.

The CNAA publishes an annual directory of approved degree, DipHE and certificate courses. This is obtainable free at present from the CNAA, 344–354 Gray's Inn Road, London WC1 8BP, though a small charge may be introduced for the 1989/90 directory.

Diploma of Higher Education

The DipHE is intended to be both a qualification in its own right and an alternative route towards a degree. If you have not made a firm decision about a career, two years of broadly based study for a DipHE give you time to work at various subjects and make up your mind later on. The courses are offered at polytechnics and colleges of higher education and some universities, and must be validated by the CNAA or by a university.

You can usually decide towards the end of the second year whether to leave with a Diploma (after successfully completing the exams) or to continue for another one or two years, working for a first degree.

Art and Design Courses

If you want to work in the art department of an advertising agency, or perhaps on design and packaging in a company, you can take a degree or vocational course in art and design; three-dimensional design; textile and fashion design; fine art. You would need to consider a course offering options in graphic design, and several colleges offer special options in media and communications design. Degree courses lead to CNAA degrees.

Art and Design Courses in Scotland

Scottish colleges now offer CNAA degrees in art and design, except Edinburgh College of Art whose degrees are validated by Heriot-Watt University. Scottish degree courses normally take four years, the first year being equivalent to a Foundation Course.

SCOTVEC offers a full-time or part-time course for a National Certificate in Graphic Design for school-leavers.

BTEC Courses in Art and Design

In order to make sure that vocational courses in art and design meet national standards of technical and professional competence, the Design Board of the Business and Technician Education Council (BTEC) supervises courses run by colleges and polytechnics all over the country. These now follow the basic pattern of two types of course and two levels; National Certificate and National Diploma; and Higher National Certificate and Higher National Diploma. The Certificate and Diploma courses are on the same academic level but the Diploma courses cover a wider range of topics and give more emphasis to management skills. All the courses can be taken on a full-time, sandwich, or day-release basis and would normally take two years full-time to complete, except for part-time Diploma and Higher Diploma courses which take three years. BTEC courses are grounded in practical and professional skills that it is hoped will make the students useful to an employer – a 'survival kit for working in the professional world' as one BTEC officer described them.

Several colleges offer BTEC courses in graphic design for advertising and communications. You can, for example, take a BTEC National Diploma course at the Newcastle College of Arts and Technology in Design (Advertising) which includes options in art direction, copywriting and work experience placements. Ealing College of Higher Education offers a two-year HND in Business and Finance (media, design and communication studies) with broad-based training in media and design within a business context; Newcastle upon Tyne Polytechnic offers a three-year HND in business studies and design for careers in marketing, advertising and publicity with option in design for visual communication. Other BTEC courses in communications may include as subjects: video production, electronic imagery, animation and film, photography, or audiovisual design.

All Art and Design courses are listed in the Design Council publication *Design Courses in Britain*, available from the Design Council, 28 Haymarket, London SW1Y 4YU, price £6.95 plus £1.90 postage and packing.

BTEC Higher National Diploma in Graphic Design/Multi-disciplinary Design

These are normally two-year full-time courses in different aspects of design, including graphic communication, and many colleges offer specialisms in advertising or allied subjects.

Business Studies

BTEC Courses in Business and Finance

The Business and Technician Education Council provides education and training for people in work, and preparing for work. BTEC offers awards at three levels: First, National and Higher National. These consist of:

First Certificates and Diplomas
National Certificates and Diplomas
Higher National Certificates and Diplomas

Each is designated to provide vocational education at the appropriate level, and consists of a common core of subjects, along with various subject options, which you choose according to your work and interests. The qualifications are nationally recognised and can lead on to further education and training. There is also a range of Continuing Education and courses for adults.

The Business and Finance courses offer a wide range of choices in every aspect of business and office work. These include advertising, marketing, marketing with languages, communications, and media studies. BTEC emphasises the importance of work experience, or simulated work experience in college, for all business education courses. It prefers full-time courses to include suitable arrangements for work experience and insists that a significant proportion of study time is devoted to simulations of work situations, case studies, business games etc.

BTEC First Certificates and Diplomas in Business and Finance

These courses provide an introduction to business studies for people wanting to work in commercial, financial, manufacturing or service organisations, or planning to do further business or computer studies. The courses aim to develop communication, numerical, information-processing and problem-solving skills, and include the core unit Working in Organisations. The certificate has two additional option units; the Diploma has five additional units.

The Diploma takes one year full-time, two years part-time; the Certificate takes one year part-time.

BTEC National Certificates and Diplomas in Business and Finance

The basic themes of these courses are: The Organisation in its Environment, Finance, and People in Organisations. For the Diploma course you have to choose seven options which can include marketing; for the Certificate course you choose three vocational options. The Diploma course takes two years full-time, three years sandwich, or three years part-time; the Certificate course takes two years part-time.

BTEC Higher National Certificates and Diplomas in Business and Finance

BTEC gives guidance about the structure of Higher National Award courses to colleges, who then devise their own courses. Each course consists of eight core units and a choice of option modules, and covers the four main study areas:

People
Communications
Money and Resources
Analysis/Numeracy/Technology

To obtain the Higher National Certificate you must complete ten units, and for the Diploma you must complete 16 units. The Certificate course lasts two years part-time; the Diploma course two years full-time, three years on a sandwich basis.

BTEC stresses that it is vital to its philosophy that even for full-time and most particularly for part-time students some studies specifically related to day-to-day vocationally relevant student activity should begin in the first year.

Full details about all BTEC courses may be obtained from BTEC Information Services.

SCOTVEC Courses in Business Studies

SCOTVEC, the Scottish Vocational Education Council, now offers four categories of award in business studies and distribution:

National Certificate
Higher National Certificate
Higher National Diploma
Diploma in Industrial Administration

National Certificate

The Scottish National Certificate is a unified qualification for all post-16 education and training in Scotland apart from the Scottish Higher Grade Certificate of Education and Certificate of Sixth Year Studies. It is a modular course, made up of units of study of about 40 hours each. They can be taken in schools, FE colleges, as part of TVEI and YTS schemes on a full-time or part-time basis. There are over 1200 modules to choose from, though not all of these will be available at every school or college. Advice can be given about which modules to take to equip you for particular careers and exemptions from professional and technical qualifications.

Someone interested in marketing, for example, could therefore take general modules in such subjects as communication media studies etc, along with specialist subjects such as Advertising, Marketing, Public Relations. A certificate showing levels of achievement in the modules taken is given to each student at the end of the course.

Scottish Higher National Certificate in Business Studies
This is intended to broaden the outlook and experience of trainee executives, and is recognised as a useful qualification by professional bodies, and employers' organisations. It takes two years part-time and one year full-time. Candidates must pass in economics and organisational psychology, and in three other subjects, one from list A, one from list B and one more from either A or B.

List A
Business Accounting
Business Systems
Business Information

List B includes:
Advertising
Marketing
Marketing Research
Information Systems
Exporting
Modern Language
Distribution

Scottish Higher National Diploma in Business Studies
The Diploma course covers similar topics in more depth and breadth. It can be taken as a two-year full-time or three-year sandwich course. Candidates must pass in:

Economics
Business Law
Business Accounting
Business Systems I
Organisational Psychology
Business Systems II

Plus *two* subjects out of the list B options for the Scottish HNC. At least four subjects must be passed in Year One before beginning Year Two and students must successfully complete a project in the second year of the course on a subject approved by the college and by the Council. This would normally be related to the optional subjects chosen.

There are also Higher National Diplomas in Business Studies and Languages which include a marketing option.

Scottish Higher National Diploma in Communication Studies

This course provides intensive study of the communications industries, with special reference to publicity and information services, public relations, advertising and the mass media. Candidates must pass in:

Language and Practice 1 and 2
Visual Communication 1 and 2
Mass Communications
Business Environment
Psychology
Literature, Art and Society
Advertising
Marketing
Public Relations
Marketing Research
Project

Students must pass in at least five of the six first-year subjects before proceeding to Year Two.

Visual communication includes a practical element and the project will have both written and oral components.

Diploma in Industrial Administration

This is another one-year full-time course at postgraduate level, which offers students the chance to obtain a thorough knowledge of business and management skills generally, while specialising in a particular area. The specialist options include marketing. As well as the general papers, marketing students must pass marketing management and two subjects from: marketing research; international marketing; management of manpower. All students have to submit a project.

CAM Foundation Courses

CAM, the Communication, Advertising and Marketing Education Foundation Limited, is an educational charity, originally formed from the educational sections of the Advertising Association, the Institute of Practitioners in Advertising and the Institute of Public Relations. It is recognised and supported by 21 organisations in the communication and education fields and the CAM Certificates and Diplomas are nationally recognised qualifications.

CAM Certificate in Communication Studies

The Certificate covers seven subjects, which may be taken separately, six of which must be passed in order to qualify. The subjects are:

Marketing
Advertising
Public Relations
Media
Sales Promotion/Direct Marketing
Research and Behavioural Studies

Students with relevant qualifications may gain exemption on a subject-for-subject basis. The Certificate normally needs two years' part-time study. Exams take place in June each year, with a re-sit session in November for UK students.

CAM Diploma

Diplomas are awarded in three areas: management and strategy, plus two specialisms: public relations, advertising, sales promotion or direct marketing, advertising, marketing, and public relations. Three subjects are chosen from a list of 10 (five for an Honours Diploma). Study for the Diploma usually takes one year part-time, and involves much case study work. Exams are held in May every year.

Tuition

You can choose how many Certificate subjects to study for at one time, but most students take three subjects a year over two years to complete the course. There are no regulations about methods of study. You can choose from:

- correspondence courses
- part-time day or evening classes at a local college
- full-time studies
- private studies.

CAM also runs its own 'Guided Studies' scheme to help students prepare for the Certificate examinations. This scheme can be used either as extra support if you are attending a college course, or instead of a correspondence course. The scheme offers a Home Study Course, with text books, learning notes and self-help questions along with an intensive one-day seminar of instruction from leading practitioners.

Full details about the CAM Foundation scheme can be obtained from CAM Foundation.

Institute of Marketing Courses

The Institute of Marketing sponsors an educational scheme of professional study in marketing based on a combination of academic attainment and practical understanding of marketing activities.

Certificate of Marketing

The two-year part-time course covers: fundamentals of marketing; principles and practice of selling; economics for marketing; quantitative studies (statistics); English business law; behavioural aspects of marketing; financial aspects of marketing; practice of marketing. Candidates must pass in all subjects. (Failed subjects can be retaken in a subsequent examination.) Exemption may be available on a subject-for-subject basis. Exams take place in June and December.

Diploma in Marketing

The Diploma is designed for people who have passed the Certificate exams or have a postgraduate qualification in Business or Management Studies which includes Marketing, or a Business degree which includes Marketing or a BTEC or SCOTVEC HNC/HND in Business Studies with Marketing option. Students who hold or are studying for a degree or postgraduate qualification in Business Management with Marketing may obtain exemptions from up to three of the Diploma's core subjects. It will be awarded only after the necessary exam success is endorsed by at least one year's practical marketing experience.

The syllabus for the one-year, part-time Diploma course covers the following areas:

Marketing Planning and Control
Marketing Communications
International Marketing
Marketing Management

Case studies are an important element of the course. The exams are held in June and December. The Diploma course takes one year part-time study. Successful candidates are eligible for graduate membership of the Institute (G Inst M). Full membership is dependent on experience in sales and marketing management.

Tuition
Courses are provided in FE colleges, polytechnics and also by correspondence colleges. Full details about the scheme can be obtained from the Institute of Marketing.

Other Courses

There are other courses suitable for people who wish to go into marketing and similar careers, and these are briefly described below. The colleges running them will be able to give you full details about the curriculum, applications, possibilities for grants etc.

Advertising

Watford College is one of the few colleges in the country running its own specially designed courses for people in advertising. The courses are highly regarded by the advertising industry.

College Diploma in Advertising
This is a one-year full-time course for people planning an executive career in an agency or client company. You must be at least 18 and have five GCE/GCSE (grade A–C) passes and two A levels or a BTEC National award, and there is an entrance test and interview. Mature candidates with relevant experience may be considered on merit.

Postgraduate Diploma in Advertising
This is a six-month full-time concentrated version for graduates of the one-year course. It is intended for people who hope to get a job in this field, and is also used by companies as an initial training course for graduates they have already chosen for a job. You must have a university or CNAA degree, or BTEC HND in Business Studies, and must take an entrance test and interview. You apply to the Department of Business Studies for both of these courses (Watford College, Hempstead Road, Watford, Hertfordshire WD1 3EZ; 0923 57591).

College Diploma in Advertising Copywriting
This is a one-year full-time course for young people planning a

career on the creative side of advertising. You must be between 18 and 21 (unless you are a graduate or 'post-experience' student), have six GCE/GCSE passes including two at A level, and take a written assessment paper prior to interview. You apply to the Department of Art and Graphic Design at Watford College.

Communication Studies

A Level in Communication Studies

The Associated Examining Board offer an A-level exam in communication studies which may be available at local FE colleges or at school.

Film and Television Studies

In addition to the various courses offered at colleges and polytechnics, there are specialised training courses for film and television production offered at:

The London International Film School
24 Shelton Street
London WC2H 9HP
01-836 9642

The School offers a two-year diploma course in film-making, covering all aspects of production. It is privately run and funded entirely on students' fees. You must have a degree or five GCE/GCSE passes and two A-level passes or equivalent, together with technical knowledge of film processing, and some experience in film-making. Candidates must provide a script and film critique with their applications.

The School offers an animation course to people already professionally qualified in film-making, and a television production course whose aim is to equip students with the knowledge of studio techniques and procedures needed to produce simple television programmes.

The National Film and Television School
Beaconsfield Film Studios
Station Road
Beaconsfield, Buckinghamshire
0496 71234

The School receives grants from the Treasury, the British Film

Fund, the Television Fund and the BBC, but is an independent educational institution. It takes in about 25 people each year for a three-year course. Most successful applicants are graduates aged between 22 and 30, but there is no official minimum educational standard. Applicants are, however, expected to show ability in writing, direction, production or photography, and must be able to produce evidence of creative work in their chosen field.

See *Careers in Film and Video* (Kogan Page) for further information.

Marketing

Several colleges offer their own diplomas, mostly at post-graduate level, on different aspects of marketing.

Bristol Polytechnic
Diploma in Marketing. One-year full-time course, aims to provide students with a thorough understanding of marketing techniques.

Kingston Polytechnic
Diploma in Marketing. One-year full-time course, includes a study of marketing problems to develop the students' analytical capacity and problem-solving techniques.

Liverpool Polytechnic
Diploma in Marketing Management. One-year full-time, designed to consider the practical implications of marketing as a process and to identify and study underlying behavioural theories within this process.

Newcastle upon Tyne Polytechnic
Diploma in Marketing. One-year full-time course, with students developing studies in marketing management, marketing research, marketing communications and international marketing.

Sheffield City Polytechnic
MSc in Management Studies. Four-year part-time course. Initially students take economics, quantitative methods, behavioural aspects of management, marketing, finance etc, after

which they concentrate on studies in decision making, management strategy and a special subject, which may be marketing management.

Staffordshire Polytechnic
Diploma in International Marketing. One-year full-time course providing an understanding of the theory and practice of international marketing and the study of a foreign language in a commercial and marketing context. Also Postgraduate Diploma in Marketing Management.

Chapter 6

Where to Study

Choosing a Course

As you can see from the variety of courses described in Chapter 1, the choice can be bewildering. It depends very much on your abilities, academic achievements and personal preferences. Here are some points that might help you to decide what you want to do.

1. Do you have the academic qualifications for a degree or similar course? If so, you would be well advised to consider this very carefully, unless you have strong personal reasons for starting work immediately on leaving school. Although it is always possible to pick up qualifications later on, perhaps on a part-time or evening class basis, it is much easier to do this through full-time study at a college. And it is a pity to miss the fun, freedom and opportunities of student life.
2. If you decide on a degree-level course, is it better to take a course specifically related to marketing, or any degree course on a subject that interests you? This depends on how committed you are to the idea of a marketing career. Taking a degree in other subjects leaves the options open until a later stage in your life, but you may then need to spend another year after taking your first degree, obtaining some specific qualification.
3. Sandwich courses offer a compromise between full-time study and part-time study combined with employment, because periods of study are sandwiched between periods of employment. There are two basic patterns: *thick sandwich courses* - two years of study, one year of supervised work experience, final year of study; and *thin sandwich courses* - usually alternating six-month periods of work and study.

4. If you feel that your academic qualifications are not likely to fulfil the requirements for a degree-level course, but you would still like to study full-time, look at the vocational courses in art and design and other subjects, and in business studies.
5. If you decide on studying through part-time or evening courses, the amount of help and support your employer will give can be very important. So find out what concessions are made for which course, and what arrangements there are for help with fees, time off for study, block-release and day-release to attend college etc.
6. Whatever type of course you choose, you need to check carefully with the requirements of professional associations to see that the course is suitable for the career you want to take up. A useful reference book here is *British Qualifications*, published annually by Kogan Page Ltd, which should be in your local reference or careers library.

Once you have some idea of the type of course you want to follow, you need to find out something about course content and structure. You could start by looking through general reference books such as *Which Degree?*, published annually by Newpoint Ltd, the CNAA *Directory of First Degree and Diploma of Higher Education Courses*, and *The Handbook of Degree and Advanced Courses in Institutes and Colleges of Higher Education, Colleges of Education, Polytechnics and University Departments of Education.*

Specimen
college prospectus enquiry

Please send me information about entrance requirements, courses, fees, residence, etc. (word this as appropriate)

BLOCK Name ....

CAPITALS Address ....

PLEASE ....

Proposed course(s) ....

....

Proposed year of entry ....

Signed .... Date ....

These should help you to draw up a short list of colleges, and you can then write to them for a copy of their course prospectus. All you have to do is send a request to the college, addressed to the Registrar or the Admissions Officer. As they have many enquiries it helps if you enclose a self-addressed and stamped gummed label (not envelope). In the case of the universities at Cambridge, London, Oxford and Wales, write to the individual college, not the university.

Choosing a College

Although the choice of course and college tend to go together, particularly if you are studying part-time or for a particular subject, it is important to look at the college environment as well as the academic content of the syllabus. If you are already at work, it is important to consult your employers and other people at work about their views on particular colleges and courses. It is essential to check the credentials of any private college before enrolling with them, to make sure that the qualifications they offer are acceptable to employers or professional associations.

As well as reading the official prospectus, it is worth having a look at any alternative student prospectus that may be available. You can usually obtain them from the Students' Union at the college. You may need to take alternative prospectuses with a pinch of salt, but they do give a new perspective to the official information.

Talking to students on the course you are interested in can be very enlightening. An opportunity to do this may arise if you make the effort to visit some of the colleges before making up your mind which to apply to. Most colleges are very happy to welcome visitors, either to formally arranged Open Days or privately arranged visits.

If you cannot afford to travel long distances to see a college, try to visit one near your home, just to give you some idea of what a Department of Business Studies, or College of Art and Design, is like.

Chapter 7

Entrance Requirements

GCSE

As the GCSE exam has replaced GCE O level and CSE, most colleges and professional institutions will require the corresponding GCSE equivalents, illustrated by the following table:

O level	*GCSE*	*CSE*
A	A	1
B	B	1
C	C	1
D	D	2
E	E	3
	F	4
	G	5

Degree and DipHE Courses

Most colleges will expect students to have five GCE/GCSE passes, including two at A level. They will probably require your GCSE/GCE O levels to be Grade C or better. Grade 1 CSE passes are regarded as equivalent to Grade C GCSE/GCE O level. Two AS levels generally count as one A level. Other acceptable qualifications are:

- GCE in four subjects with three at A level;
- Scottish Certificate of Education with passes in three subjects, including three at Higher level;
- Scottish Certificate of Education with passes in four subjects at Higher level;
- BTEC/SCOTVEC National Certificate, Diploma or Higher National Diploma, or the equivalent qualifications;

- Other equivalent qualifications - see college prospectus for details or write to the college asking for information.

You need to look very carefully at the entrance requirements for the course you wish to take. Courses in business studies normally require GCSE/GCE O-level mathematics and often O-level English language or equivalent. Courses with a language content will ask for the appropriate language qualification.

University Entrance: The Official Guide which should be in your local reference library or school careers library, will give you information about all university courses. Information about requirements for other advanced courses is given briefly in:

> *A Compendium of Advanced Courses in Colleges of Further and Higher Education*, published by the Regional Advisory Councils in England and Wales and available from The London and South-Eastern Regional Advisory Council for Further Education, Tavistock House South, Tavistock Square, London WC1H 9LR, and

> *The Handbook of Degree and Advanced Courses in Institutions, Colleges of Higher Education, Polytechnics and University Departments of Education*, published by NATFHE/Linneys ESL, 121 Newgate Lane, Mansfield, Nottinghamshire NG18 2PA.

Be sure to use the most recent edition of all these books, and then check with the college prospectus. Applying for a course for which you are not qualified is a very common mistake.

The requirements listed are the *minimum* needed to qualify, and when a course is very popular, the standard may be considerably higher. Brian Heap's *Degree Course Offers*, which should be in the reference library, can give you some idea of the standard prevailing at different colleges. He lists the various offers made to candidates applying for degree courses at UK universities and polytechnics.

Art and Design Courses

Foundation Courses

Many colleges prefer students to have taken a foundation course before embarking on a degree course in art and design.

Foundation courses may last for one or two years, depending on your age when you begin. Normally, students take a one-year course, and must be at least 17 and have five GCSE/GCE O-level passes at Grade C or better. For a two-year course, beginning a year earlier at 16, three GCSE passes may be acceptable, and students continue with GCSE studies during their first year.

Degree Courses

Normal minimum requirements are one of the following:

(a) GCE/GCSE passes in five subjects, including two subjects at A level; *or*
(b) GCE/GCSE passes in four subjects including three subjects at A level; *or*
(c) A Scottish Certificate of Education (SCE) with passes in five subjects, of which three are at the Higher (H) grade; *or*
(d) An SCE with passes in four subjects, all at H grade; *or*
(e) BTEC/SCOTVEC National Certificate or Diploma at a good standard; *or*
(f) The satisfactory completion of a full-time foundation course in art and design of not less than one year, together with one of the following:

    (i) GCE passes in five subjects at O level, or GCSE equivalent, *or*
    (ii) GCE/GCSE passes in four subjects including one at A level, *or*
    (iii) Equivalent qualifications.

Colleges do have discretion to admit small numbers of students who do not have the stipulated academic qualifications, if they feel that the student has the creative ability to profit from the course. The CNAA stress, however, that they feel a foundation course is the best way of demonstrating and testing creative ability, and that this should be the normal qualification for entry.

BTEC Courses in Design

Colleges are asked to keep the entrance requirements fairly flexible, but a minimum of four CSEs at Grade 3 or four GCSE/GCE O-level passes would normally be required for the National Certificate and Diploma courses. For the Higher National Certificate or Higher National Diploma, a BTEC Certificate or Diploma is acceptable. An alternative is GCE A levels or their equivalent, in which case some candidates may be asked to undertake some bridging study to fill in any gaps.

Scottish Degree Courses

Courses normally require at least five Scottish Certificate of Education passes with three at Higher level, or equivalent.

BTEC Courses

BTEC First Awards

Students must be 16 years of age and have left school. No formal exam passes are needed but they must satisfy the college that they have the potential to benefit from the course.

BTEC National Certificate and Diplomas

As well as the above requirements, students must have at least one of the following:

1. A BTEC First Certificate/Diploma;
2. CPVE;
3. Four GCSE/GCE O-level passes at Grade C or better;
4. Four CSE Grade 1 passes;
5. A qualification which BTEC accepts as equivalent to any of the above, such as a Foundation Programme with appropriate attainments.

Colleges may admit students of 19 and over without the minimum entry requirements but with relevant experience. Their details must be sent in to BTEC when they are registered.

BTEC Higher National Awards

You must normally be 18 years of age. For courses in Design, selection is normally by interview and centres will ask to see examples of previous work as evidence of imagination and potential. You must also have at least one of the following:

1. BTEC National Certificate/Diploma;
2. Suitable A/AS-level passes;
3. Any other qualification accepted by BTEC as equivalent.

Students over 21 may, exceptionally, be accepted without the minimum entry requirements, provided that BTEC are notified when they register. Requirements depend on the individual course.

Conversion Courses

Colleges can arrange bridging studies or a conversion programme for A-level entrants and people taking a BTEC course.

SCOTVEC Courses

National Certificate

Students must be 16 years old, and can choose from over 2,500 subject modules, each taking 40 hours. They can be combined with O-grade, standard-grade and H-grade studies.

Higher National Certificate or Diploma in Business Studies

Completion of an appropriate National Certificate programme in relevant interdisciplinary studies, such as Media or Creative and Aesthetic Studies modules; or equivalent; *or*

appropriate group of SCE O- and H-grade passes, or GCSE/GCE O levels and A levels; or equivalent; *or*

for candidates over 21, other equivalent qualifications at the discretion of the college principal.

Diploma in Industrial Administration

Candidates must have a university or CNAA degree or an HND or equivalent qualification.

CAM Foundation Courses

Students for the Certificate and Diplomas must be registered with CAM. Students must be registered by 20 February in order to be allowed to sit the exams that year.

Certificate Courses

Students must be at least 18 and meet *one* of the following criteria:

1. Hold any UK degree or five GCE/GCSE passes including English language, two of which must be at A level; *or*
2. BTEC/SCOTVEC National Certificate/Diploma in Business Studies; *or*
3. London Chamber of Commerce and Industry Third Level Group Diploma in Marketing, Advertising or Public Relations; *or*
4. International Advertising Association Basic Certificate in Advertising; *or*
5. Have been in full-time employment in a relevant part of the communication business for a minimum of one year and have five GCSE/GCE passes at O level including English language;

6. In special circumstances students who have been in the business for at least three years can be accepted with fewer academic qualifications, providing they have the recommendation of their employer or college principal.

Diploma Courses

Candidates must either hold or be exempted from the CAM Certificate in all six subjects, although they may register for study for the Diploma when they have passed five out of the six.

Exemptions may be available on a subject-for-subject basis. Full exemption may be granted to holders of the Institute of Marketing Diploma or BTEC/SCOTVEC Awards, degrees or postgraduate qualifications in relevant subjects. Apply to the CAM Foundation registrar for further details.

Institute of Marketing Courses

All students must be registered with the Institute before they can enter for the examinations.

Certificate

You must be at least 18 and have one of the following qualifications:

1. Five GCE/GCSE (or equivalent) passes, including one at A level, and evidence of proficiency in numeracy and English;
2. BTEC/SCOTVEC National Certificate or Diploma in Business Studies;
3. One year or more of full-time marketing experience and four GCSE/GCE O-level passes.

Applicants aged 21 or over who satisfy none of the foregoing may be accepted on an age plus experience basis.

Diploma

You must have one of the following qualifications:

1. Institute of Marketing Certificate;
2. A postgraduate Diploma in Marketing or Management Studies (with IM-approved marketing module);
3. A degree or postgraduate degree in a business-related subject (with an IM-approved marketing module);
4. Any other UK degree, which may be considered providing the applicant has passed the 'Financial Aspects of Market-

ing' and the 'Practice of Marketing' IM Certificate subjects or have an equivalent qualification;

5. An approved BTEC or SCOTVEC Higher Diploma or Certificate award in business studies which includes an IM-approved marketing option;
6. Any other recognised equivalent qualifications which may be approved by the Institute.

Certain equivalent qualifications may also obtain subject-for-subject exemption. If there is any doubt, candidates should send full details of their working experience (name and address of employer or business, an outline of duties and responsibilities, and an indication of areas of authority) to the Academic Registrar, Institute of Marketing, whose decision will be final.

Mature Students

Most colleges will give special consideration to people who left school some years before, and have now decided that they would like to take a further course but do not have all the required entry qualifications. Write to the college in which you are interested, setting out your interests, experience and the qualifications you have. You will probably have to undergo a searching interview and may be asked to take a test of attainment, or perhaps a preliminary course of study to prepare you for the return to full-time education.

A booklet *Mature Students and Universities* is available free of charge from UCCA.

Some of the Open University courses may be very suitable as a preparation for full-time study, and the CNAA have special arrangements for people with OU qualifications and credits.

The CAM Foundation, Institute of Marketing and BTEC courses are all prepared to relax entry requirements for people who have worked in advertising or marketing for some time, if their experience is considered relevant and suitable.

Chapter 8

How to Apply for Courses and Training

University Degree Courses

All applications for degree courses at universities throughout the United Kingdom have to go through UCCA - the Universities Central Council on Admissions. The only exceptions are Cranfield Institute of Technology, the Open University and the University of Buckingham. Full details about how to apply for a university first-degree course, including the complex arrangements for Oxford and Cambridge are set out in the very clear and precise *UCCA How to apply for admission to a university*, obtainable free from UCCA.

Briefly, you choose five universities and list them on your UCCA form. You can mark your preferred university with an asterisk. You also give details of your academic qualifications. Some universities will lay down general 'matriculation' requirements for all students regardless of the course, so make sure that your qualifications satisfy these as well as the ones required by the course. There have been cases where a student accepted by a department has been rejected by the university on these grounds.

There are two other important parts of the form - a space for you to describe your interests and activities, and a space for your school or college to write a confidential report on you. With so many well qualified candidates, these two personal descriptions are often very important in helping university admission tutors to select candidates.

You return the forms to UCCA and they are then sent to your chosen universities, who decide whether or not to interview you, or make you an offer without interview. An offer may be conditional, ie dependent on your obtaining certain grades at A level, or unconditional. You are allowed to hold a maximum of two offers at any one time.

Important dates are:

1 September	- Opening date for applications.
Mid October	- Closing date for Oxford and Cambridge entries.
Mid-December	- Closing date for all other entries.

The earlier you get your entry in, the better.

After January the Continuing Application Procedure begins to operate, to help those who fail to receive any offers from their first five choices. They get the chance to apply again to universities whose courses still have vacancies. Then in August and September, after the A-level results are out, the Clearing Operation takes place. People who have no offers at that stage, or have failed to get the required grades for their conditional offers, are given another chance to apply for vacancies - UCCA estimates that about 8.7 per cent of places are finally allocated at this stage and about one-third of those who apply for clearing get a place, so it is not a forlorn hope.

Art and Design Courses

Foundation and Vocational Courses

You should write to your local education authority at the Education Offices in the first place, asking for details of their courses, and then apply direct to the colleges in which you are interested. You will probably be called for an interview and asked to bring a portfolio of work.

Your school or college will almost certainly be asked by the college for a confidential statement about your interests and abilities, and this will be very important when they are making their choice of candidates. If for any reason you would prefer someone else to give this reference, you must make sure that they are of appropriate professional status.

CNAA Degree in Art and Design

For all courses at degree level and for BTEC Higher National Diploma Courses in design, except for colleges in Scotland, you must apply through the Art and Design Admissions Registry (ADAR).

Application Forms

If you are taking a foundation course at a school or college, you must obtain an application form for the ADAR scheme through your school or college. If you are at secondary school you should obtain the forms through your headteacher.

If you are not at a school, art college or further education college, ie an external candidate, you can write direct to the ADAR Registry for forms; enclose a large stamped addressed envelope (9½ × 6½ in) and the fee of £5.

Applications

1. You must complete forms APP1 and APP2 for CNAA degree courses or forms APP10 and APP11 for BTEC HND courses, and give a first and second choice of college, and the area of study you are interested in.
2. You then pass the forms to your college or school headteacher, so that the confidential report can be completed. You also give to the headteacher the fee of £5 to be sent on to the Registry. External candidates must arrange for someone suitable to complete this report.
3. Your school or college headteacher will then send form APP1 or APP10 to your first choice college, and form APP2 or APP11 to the Registry. External candidates should ask the person completing their report to send form APP10 direct to the first choice college, and should send form APP2 or APP11 direct to the Registry themselves.

Selection

Colleges will decide which first-choice applicants to interview and may ask for portfolios to be submitted in advance of an interview.

The colleges must make up their minds by mid-May which first choice candidates they will offer places to. They must send on the forms of rejected candidates to the second-choice colleges.

Colleges must decide by early June which second-choice candidates they will accept, and must return the forms of rejected candidates to the Registry.

The Registry will then send a list of vacancies, with application forms, to candidates who have not yet obtained a place. If you want to apply for any of these vacancies you send the form direct to the college.

Late Applications

Applications will be accepted after 25 March only in exceptional circumstances. You should write direct to the Registry, with the £5 fee.

Timetable (1989)

January	Requests for application forms should be made to school, college or Registry.
1 February	The Registry begin to distribute forms.
31 March	Closing date for forms to be submitted to first-choice colleges and to Registry.
1 April	Interviewing first-choice candidates begins.
9 May	Colleges must notify first-choice candidates whether or not they are successful before this date.
16 May	Second-choice interviewing begins.
5 June	Colleges must notify second-choice candidates whether or not they are successful before this date.
16 June	Unsuccessful candidates receive vacancy list.
23 June	Interviewing of 'pool' candidates begins.

Art and Design Courses in Scotland

The Scottish Art Colleges do not participate in the ADAR scheme, so for any course at a Scottish college you must apply direct to the college. The prospectus will give you details of how to do this. Apply as early as possible, as popular courses are bound to fill up early in the year.

Polytechnic Central Admissions System (PCAS)

All other degree and DipHE courses at polytechnics now use PCAS, a centralised system on UCCA lines. The PCAS *Guide for Applicants*, published in June each year, gives all the details of how to apply. Applicants fill in one form naming four courses, with no order of preference. These are sent simultaneously to the polytechnics named, who make either a conditional or unconditional offer or reject the application. Candidates may not hold more than two offers.

Important Dates

15 December	Normal closing date.
31 March	Deadline for offers.
15 May	Candidates holding two offers decide between main and 'insurance' offer.
September	Clearing procedure.

You still have to apply direct to the individual polytechnic if you wish to apply for a course that is not included in PCAS. The college prospectus will advise about this.

The PCAS guide is available free from PCAS.

Other Courses

The other courses mentioned in this book do not have a clearing-house system of application like UCCA/PCAS and the Art and Design Admissions Registry, apart from some DipHE courses at colleges mainly concerned with courses in education. You may have to apply for these through the Central Register and Clearing House scheme for teaching qualifications. This will be explained in the college prospectus. Otherwise, you apply direct to the college concerned, according to the instructions given in the college prospectus.

There probably will not be a closing date for applications because most colleges continue accepting applications until the course is full. But popular courses fill up fast, so you should apply as early as you can in the academic year before you want to begin the course. It is important to read the college's instructions carefully, and fill in the form neatly and accurately. If you are asked for a personal statement about yourself, your interests and why you want to take that particular course, compose this with care. Do not make claims about yourself and your interests that you cannot substantiate, but try to make it interesting and lively. Try to keep to the length they suggest - not too long and not too short.

You will be asked to name at least one person who can give a reference about your academic work. Most people will ask their school or college to give this reference, but if you prefer to ask someone else, it is best to explain your reasons to the college. Make sure you choose someone of appropriate status and experience.

There are various schemes to help people who have difficulty in finding a place, especially towards the end of the summer. The Higher Education Information Centre offers free advice on all types of higher education. The use of a computer means that up-to-date information on courses is available for answering queries, and the Centre has an extensive library of careers and examination information as well as the prospectuses of colleges in the UK. Anyone can contact the Centre for advice at the Middlesex Polytechnic, Bramley Road, Oakwood, London N14 4XS; 01-368 1299.

The Educational Counselling and Credit Transfer Information Service (ECCTIS) also provides a comprehensive source of information about the courses available in further and higher education on a compact disc playable on a personal computer linked to a CD ROM player - which may be in your school careers department; also on Prestel.

The Advanced Further Education Service (AFEIS) is now run by the Polytechnic Central Admissions System (PCAS). In August and September, polytechnics and colleges supply the AFEIS office with lists of vacancies in their full-time courses. AFEIS circulates these lists to local Careers Advisory Officers, who are normally based in local education authority careers offices. Schools and individuals can contact the advisory officers for the latest information and advice.

The scheme does not cover art and design courses, university degrees, or teacher education courses, all of which have their own systems for late vacancies.

This service is used by the Higher Education Information Centre in co-operation with the *Observer* newspaper every summer when the exam results come out, to give help and advice to people looking for places. The *Sunday Times* also prints useful information at that time of year about courses and vacancies.

Interviews

Colleges, and individual departments within a college, vary in their interviewing policy. Some interview everyone; some interview a short-list of most likely candidates; some interview borderline cases. Some will offer an interview only after they have offered you a place. So you should be prepared for an interview, although it may not be significant if you are not called for one.

It is a good idea to get someone to give you a mock interview, so that you can practise interviewing techniques and be warned against some of the more obvious faults. Remember that an interview is an opportunity for you to find out more about the course and the college, as well as for the college to get to know you. Take any chance of looking round the buildings and halls of residence to try to meet students, even if this is not specifically arranged for you. It may be worth writing to the Students' Union in advance to ask for their help.

It is best to play safe and dress conventionally, even though dress is less formal nowadays. Think beforehand about your answers to stock questions such as, 'Why do you want to come here?' 'What interests you about marketing?' but do not learn answers parrot-fashion and drag them in regardless of the question. Don't pretend to know the answer if you are not sure, but try to respond positively.

You are planning a career in an occupation based on the need to explain and project information. Here is the first product you have to demonstrate - yourself - so prepare for the interview carefully, and do not be intimidated.

Students with a Disability

Most colleges are prepared to do their best to make special arrangements for students with a handicap. Before making a formal application, it is sensible to write to the college in which you are interested, explaining what your particular difficulties are and asking its advice.

Skill: National Bureau for Students with Disabilities publishes a series of leaflets giving helpful information about various aspects of study with a handicap, and is hoping to prepare a handbook on applying to college for disabled students. The Bureau can also give information about the colleges which have special facilities and purpose-built accommodation. Write to the Information Service, Skill: National Bureau for Students with Disabilities, 336 Brixton Road, London SW9 7AA; 01-274 0565, if you have any problems.

Chapter 9
Fees and Grants

Degree-Level Courses

If you are accepted for a first-degree course at a UK institution or a similar course certified by the DES to be equivalent to a first degree, and have lived in Great Britain for at least three years, you should be eligible for a grant. Courses accepted by the DES as equivalent to degree courses include BTEC and SCOTVEC Higher National Diplomas, teacher training courses, and DipHE courses. Grants for degree students are mandatory and paid on a means-tested national scale. If you have been self-supporting for at least three years you can claim a grant means-tested according to your income, not your parents'; otherwise the scale of grant varies according to your parents' income.

In England and Wales grants are paid by the local education authority, in Scotland through the Education Department, and in Northern Ireland on a similar basis to England and Wales.

A full grant is supposed to cover the tuition fees, college dues, student union fees, plus an allowance for board and lodging during term and Christmas and Easter vacations, books, equipment and travel.

Full details about grants are given in the DES leaflet *Grants for Students, a Brief Guide*, available free from DES Information Division, Elizabeth House, York Road, London SE1 7PH and, for Scottish students, *Guide to Student Allowances* from the Scottish Education Department, Awards Branch, Haymarket House, Clifton Terrace, Edinburgh EH12 5DT.

In Northern Ireland, a similar leaflet is available from the Department of Education, Scholarships Branch, Rathgael House, Balloo Road, Bangor, County Down BT19 2PR.

Grants for DipHE Students

As the DipHE is a designated course, LEAs must pay a student grant for it. If you decide to transfer to a first-degree course the LEA must pay a grant covering the full course, a total of three years for an ordinary degree or four years for some honours degrees. Problems sometimes occur if the total length of time you are studying is more than three (or four) years. LEAs do not have to pay grants for the extra time, though many of them choose to do so. At a time when LEAs are having to make cuts in educational expenditure it may be more difficult to get 'topping-up' grants. So you may have to support yourself for one year of the course if you are taking more than the normal period to complete it.

Applications

You should be able to get the appropriate forms from your school or college, or direct from the LEA or Education Department.

It is a good idea to put in a preliminary application for a grant as soon as you make up your mind that you will be taking some kind of course. You can then get all the necessary forms and evidence of parents' income etc ready in advance, even if you have not yet received a firm offer of a place. Do not leave the grant application until the last minute, as the offices are very busy at the end of the summer and your application may be delayed. This means you could be faced with large bills to pay at the beginning of term, and no grant to pay them with.

Because the amount of grant you receive depends on your parents' income, it is essential to have their co-operation in preparing the application form. Some students have had difficulties either because their parents refuse to give details of their income or because they are unwilling, or unable, to pay the parental contribution towards the costs of studying at college which the national scales of payment expect.

LEAs will pay only tuition fees to students whose parents have not completed the income statement on the application form, but nothing towards maintenance. If you do run into this kind of difficulty, your school or college tutor may be able to help by discussing the problem with your parents. Unfortunately, there is no scheme to help students whose parents do not support them.

Grants for Other Courses

LEAs have the power to pay grants, known as discretionary grants, for courses below degree level, but there are no national scales or regulations. You should write to your local education authority to find out whether you would be eligible for any financial help. These discretionary grants may be hard to get in times of education cuts, but it is always worth trying.

If you live in Scotland or Northern Ireland, you apply to your education authority for these grants, not to the national education department.

If you are studying part-time for a professional qualification, your employer may be prepared to give you some help, perhaps in paying fees or allowing time off with pay.

Private Students

Some colleges will accept private students, who are not eligible for any kind of grant. You should make it clear on your application form if you come into this category, and you will be asked to provide evidence that you have the resources needed.

The cost of fees for home students ranges from around £600 to just under £1,900 (1989/90 rates) depending on the level of the course. Overseas students may have to pay up to three or four times as much as this. Board and lodging could cost over £2,000 a year, and you would also need pocket money, money for books and travel and holiday expenses.

People with a Disability

In addition to the normal grants, students with a handicap can claim the disabled student's allowance, if the handicap means that they incur extra expense when going to college. The maximum paid is £730 a year. Students on degree-level courses are entitled to this allowance by right if they qualify; students on other courses are usually, but not always, given extra grants on the same basis as degree students.

Skill: National Bureau for Students with Disabilities can give help and advice on applying for grants, and publishes a very useful free leaflet *Financial Assistance for Students with Disabilities* setting out details about grants and other financial help.

Chapter 10

Colleges Providing Courses

This chapter contains the information needed to find out which colleges offer the courses in which you are interested. Where a large number of colleges offer the same course, we give the best source for obtaining a full list of the relevant institutions. If a course is offered by only a few colleges, brief details are given of the course content together with the college name and address.

University Degree Courses

Many universities offer courses for degrees in business studies or management studies. The *UCCA How to apply for admission to a university* will identify them for you, and you then need to check very carefully with the college prospectus to see whether the course suits you. Most of them will have some marketing content.

The following university courses in other subjects would also be of interest to people intending to take up a career in marketing or advertising.

Marketing

Aberystwyth
BSc Econ Hons in Economics and Marketing
BSc Hons in Agricultural and Food Marketing

Cranfield Institute of Technology
Bsc Hons in Rural Resources Management, special subject Food Marketing and Distribution

Lancaster
BSc Hons course in Management Sciences (Marketing)

BA Hons course in Art, Design and Marketing; and Marketing with French or German

Newcastle upon Tyne
BSc Hons in Agricultural and Food Marketing

Reading
BSc Hons in Food Manufacture, Management and Marketing; and Food Science, Food Economics and Marketing

Salford
BSc Hons Modern Languages and Marketing Studies

Stirling
BA Hons French/Marketing

Strathclyde
BA Joint Hons Marketing and a language
BA Joint Honours: two from a choice of subjects including Marketing; Management Science; Modern Languages; Psychology; Administration; Economics; Business Law
BSc Hons in Technology and Business Studies - one technology subject plus a business subject from a choice including marketing

Communications Studies

Bradford
Interdisciplinary Human Studies - has a communications option

Brunel
BSc four-year Honours Course: Communication and Information Studies

Goldsmiths' College, London
BA Honours course Communications Studies and Sociology

Film Studies
Several universities offer film studies - see UCCA handbook. Many of these courses are concerned with film appreciation, not with techniques of film production. Check with the prospectus before you apply.

Typography and Graphic Design

Reading
BA Hons in Typography and Graphic Communication

CNAA Degree Courses

You can find full details of all CNAA degrees and DipHE courses in the *Directory of First Degree and Diploma of Higher Education Courses* published by CNAA, available free. Most CNAA degrees in Business Studies offer a marketing option.

Some other degrees that might be useful are:

Huddersfield Polytechnic
BA Hons in Textile Marketing. Four-year thick sandwich course.
BA Hons in Marketing (Engineering). Four-year thick sandwich course, providing an education in marketing allied to an understanding of the problems, processes and technology of the engineering industry, with particular relevance to either electrical engineering or mechanical engineering.

Polytechnic of East London
BA Hons in Manufacturing Systems Management. Four-year sandwich course.

Paisley College of Technology
BA, BA Hons in Business Information Technology (with Finance, Marketing or General Management). Four- to five-year thick sandwich course.

Sheffield City Polytechnic
BSc Hons in Food Marketing Sciences. Four-year thin sandwich course.

Thames Polytechnic
BA, BA Hons in International Marketing. Four-year thick sandwich course, offering an in-depth coverage of marketing with substantial language studies in French, German or Spanish.

Communication Studies

These are multi-disciplinary courses, which include studies in sociology, psychology and linguistics, and the relationship between culture and society. They may be of interest to people looking for careers in advertising, public relations and marketing, but do not provide professional training.

Film and Photography Studies
In addition to specialist courses in film and photography, these are often offered as an option in multi-disciplinary courses. Check with the CNAA *Directory* and check the college prospectus for details of course content.

Art and Design Courses

The best source of information about art and design courses is the Design Council publication *Design Courses in Britain* which lists the different kinds of course available all over the country. Available from the Design Council (details on page 50).

Information about art and design degrees is given in the CNAA Directory *First Degree and Diploma of Higher Education Courses.*

BTEC Courses

Information about colleges offering BTEC courses is available from the Business and Technician Education Council, Central House, Upper Woburn Place, London WC1H 0HH; 01-388 3288, which can give you a list of colleges offering BEC courses with the options available. Information about Higher Diploma courses is also given in the *Compendium of Advanced Courses in Colleges of Further and Higher Education*, published by the Regional Advisory Councils.

SCOTVEC Courses

National Certificate and Diploma courses are available at many FE centres in Scotland, and you should be able to find out from your education authority where they are offered in your area.

Further information can be obtained from the Publicity/ Public Relations Department, SCOTVEC, Hanover House, 24 Douglas Street, Glasgow G2 7NQ; 041-248 7900.

CAM Foundation Courses

The CAM prospectus lists all colleges offering courses in the United Kingdom and abroad, and accredited correspondence colleges. Available from CAM Foundation, Abford House, 15 Wilton Road, London SW1V 1NJ; 01-828 7506.

Institute of Marketing Courses

Details of colleges offering courses are available from the Institute, Moor Hall, Cookham, Maidenhead, Berkshire SL6 9QH; 06285 24922.

Correspondence Courses

There are all kinds of reasons for preferring to study by correspondence course rather than attend a college. There may be no suitable course available locally; you may wish to begin half-way through the academic year; you may not want to give up the same evening every week to attend classes; you may just prefer working on your own. However, it is more difficult to study independently without the support of other students and the stimulus of going to lectures and classes, so you need to be fairly well-organised to succeed.

If you do decide to take a correspondence course, make sure that the course is approved by your employers, or the professional organisations, and that the college offering the course is endorsed by the Council for the Accreditation of Correspondence Colleges. A list of accredited colleges is in the *Education Yearbook* which should be in your local reference library. The Institute of Sales and Marketing Management, Georgian House, 31 Upper George Street, Luton LU1 2RD offers a Diploma in Sales Management by correspondence course through the Institute's Educational Division.

Chapter 11

Useful Addresses

Please note that from 6 May 1990 London telephone numbers will no longer have the 01- local area code. Instead numbers will start with either 071- or 081-. Readers should check with British Telecom after 6 May 1990 if in doubt.

Art and Design Admissions Registry (ADAR)
Penn House
9 Broad Street
Hereford HR4 9AP
0432 266653

Business and Technician Education Council (BTEC)
Information Services
Central House
Upper Woburn Place
London WC1H 0HH
01-388 3288

CAM Foundation
Abford House
15 Wilton Road
London SW1V 1NJ
01-828 7506

Council for National and Academic Awards (CNAA)
344–354 Gray's Inn Road
London WC1 8BP
01-278 4411

Department of Education and Science (DES)
Information Division
Elizabeth House
York Road
London SE1 7PH
01-934 9000

Department of Education, Northern Ireland
Scholarships Branch
Rathgael House
Balloo Road
Bangor
Co Down BT19 2PR
0247 466311

Design Council
28 Haymarket
London SW1Y 4YU
01-839 8000

Designers and Art Directors Association
12 Carlton House Terrace
London SW1Y 5AH
01-839 2964

Higher Education Information Centre
Middlesex Polytechnic
Bramley Road
Oakwood
London N14 4XS
01-368 1299

Institute of Marketing
Moor Hall
Cookham
Maidenhead
Berkshire SL6 9QH
06285 24922

Institute of Practitioners in Advertising
44 Belgrave Square
London SW1X 8QS
01-235 7020

Institute of Public Relations
Gate House
St John's Square
London EC1M 4DH
01-253 5151

Institute of Sales and Marketing Management
Georgian House
31 Upper George Street
Luton
Bedfordshire LU1 2RD
0582 411130

London and Regional Advisory Council for Education
Tavistock House South
Tavistock Square
London WC1H 9LR
01-388 0027

London International Film School
24 Shelton Street
London WC2H 9HP
01-836 9642

NATFHE/Linneys ESL
121 Newgate Lane
Mansfield
Nottinghamshire NG18 2PA
0623 656565

National Film and Television School
Beaconsfield Film Studios
Station Road
Beaconsfield
Buckinghamshire
0496 71234

Polytechnic Central Admissions System (PCAS)
PO Box 67
Cheltenham
Gloucestershire GL50 3AP
0242 526225

Scottish Education Department
Awards Branch
Haymarket House
Clifton Terrace
Edinburgh EH12 5DT
031-556 8400

Scottish Vocational Education Council (SCOTVEC)
Hanover House
24 Douglas Street
Glasgow G2 7NQ
041-248 7900

Skill: National Bureau for Students with Disabilities
336 Brixton Road
London SW9 7AA
01-274 0565

Universities Central Council on Admissions (UCCA)
PO Box 28
Cheltenham
Gloucestershire GL50 1HY
0242 222444

The Kogan Page Careers Series

This series consists of short guides (96-160 pages) to different careers for school and college leavers, graduates and anyone wanting to start anew. Each book serves as an introduction to a particular career and to jobs available within that field, including full details of training qualifications and courses. The following 'Careers in' titles are available in paperback.

Accountancy *(3rd edition)*
Alternative Medicine *(2nd edition)*
Antiques
Architecture *(2nd edition)*
Art and Design *(5th edition)*
Aviation
Banking and Finance *(2nd edition)*
Business
Catering and Hotel Management *(3rd edition)*
The Church
Civil Engineering
Civil Service
Computing and Information Technology
Conservation *(3rd edition)*
Crafts
Dance
Electrical and Electronic Engineering *(2nd edition)*
Engineering *(3rd edition)*
Fashion *(2nd edition)*
Film and Video
Floristry and Retail Gardening
Hairdressing and Beauty Therapy *(4th edition)*
Holiday Industry *(2nd edition)*
Home Economics *(2nd edition)*
Journalism *(3rd edition)*
Land and Property
The Law *(4th edition)*
Librarianship and Information Science *(2nd edition)*
Marketing, Public Relations and Advertising *(3rd edition)*
Medicine, Dentistry and Mental Health *(3rd edition)*
Modelling *(2nd edition)*
Museums and Art Galleries
Music Business
Nursing and Allied Professions *(4th edition)*
Oil and Gas
Pharmacy
Photography *(2nd edition)*
Politics
Printing
Psychology
Publishing
Retailing *(3rd edition)*
Road Transport
At Sea
Secretarial and Office Work *(4th edition)*
Social Work *(3rd edition)*
Sport *(2nd edition)*
Surveying
Teaching *(2nd edition)*
Telecommunications
Television and Radio *(2nd edition)*
The Theatre *(2nd edition)*
Using Biology
Using Languages *(3rd edition)*
Using Mathematics
Veterinary Surgery
Working Abroad
Working Outdoors *(3rd edition)*
Working with Animals *(4th edition)*
Working with Children and Young People *(3rd edition)*

Also Available from Kogan Page

An A–Z of Careers and Jobs (3rd edition), edited by Diane Burston
Changing Your Job After 35: The Daily Telegraph Guide (6th edition), Godfrey Golzen and Philip Plumbley
How to Get on in Marketing, Advertising and Public Relations: A Career Development Guide, ed Norman Hart and Norman Waite
Getting There: Jobhunting for Women, Margaret Wallis
Great Answers to Tough Interview Questions: How to Get the Job You Want (2nd edition), Martin John Yate
How to Choose a Career (2nd edition), Vivien Donald
How to Get a Highly Paid Job in the City, Richard Roberts and Luke Johnson
The Kogan Page Guide to Careers in the Media, edited by Julia Allen
Making a Living as a Rock Musician, Kim Ludman
Moving On From Teaching: Career Development for Teachers, Caroline Elton
Offbeat Careers: 60 Ways to Avoid Becoming an Accountant, Vivien Donald
Working Abroad: The Daily Telegraph Guide to Working and Living Overseas (11th edition), Godfrey Golzen
Working for Yourself: The Daily Telegraph Guide to Self-Employment (10th edition), Godfrey Golzen
Working for Yourself in the Arts and Crafts (2nd edition), Sarah Hosking
Writing for a Living (2nd edition), Ian Linton

Running Your Own Antiques Business, Noël Riley and Godfrey Golzen
Running Your Own Boarding Kennels, Sheila Zabawa
Running Your Own Building Business, Kim Ludman
Running Your Own Catering Business, Ursula Garner and Judy Ridgway
Running Your Own Driving School, Nigel Stacey
Running Your Own Estate Agency, Val Redding
Running Your Own Hairdressing Salon, Christine Harvey and Helen Steadman
Running Your Own Mail Order Business, Malcolm Breckman
Running Your Own Photographic Business, John Rose and Linda Hankin
Running Your Own Pub, Elven Money

Running Your Own Restaurant, Diane Hughes and Godfrey Golzen
Running Your Own Shop (2nd edition), Roger Cox
Running Your Own Small Hotel (2nd edition), Joy Lennick
Running Your Own Typing Service, Doreen Huntley
Running Your Own Wine Bar, Judy Ridgway